Tort Law in Brazil

Tort Law in Brazil

Second Edition

Eugênio Battesini
Magnum Koury de Figueiredo Eltz
Cesar Santolim

This book was originally published as a monograph in the International Encyclopaedia of Laws/Tort Law.

Founding Editor: Roger Blanpain
General Editor: Frank Hendrickx
Volume Editor: Britt Weyts

Wolters Kluwer

Published by:
Kluwer Law International B.V.
PO Box 316
2400 AH Alphen aan den Rijn
The Netherlands
E-mail: international-sales@wolterskluwer.com
Website: www.wolterskluwer.com/en/solutions/kluwerlawinternational

Sold and distributed by:
Wolters Kluwer Legal & Regulatory U.S.
7201 McKinney Circle
Frederick, MD 21704
United States of America
E-mail: customer.service@wolterskluwer.com

DISCLAIMER: The material in this volume is in the nature of general comment only. It is not offered as advice on any particular matter and should not be taken as such. The editor and the contributing authors expressly disclaim all liability to any person with regard to anything done or omitted to be done, and with respect to the consequences of anything done or omitted to be done wholly or partly in reliance upon the whole or any part of the contents of this volume. No reader should act or refrain from acting on the basis of any matter contained in this volume without first obtaining professional advice regarding the particular facts and circumstances at issue. Any and all opinions expressed herein are those of the particular author and are not necessarily those of the editor or publisher of this volume.

Printed on acid-free paper

ISBN 978-94-035-4272-0

e-Book: ISBN 978-94-035-4273-7
web-PDF: ISBN 978-94-035-4274-4

This title is available on www.kluwerlawonline.com

Printed and bound by CPI Group (UK) Ltd, Croydon, CR0 4YY

The Authors

Eugênio Battesini was born on June 27, 1964, in the city of Canoas, Rio Grande do Sul, Brazil. He received a bachelor's degree in law in 1987 from the Pontifical Catholic University of Rio Grande do Sul, a bachelor's degree in business administration in 1991 from the Federal University of Rio Grande do Sul and a bachelor's degree in economics in 1999 from the Federal University of Rio Grande do Sul. He received a specialism in the law of the economy and business in 2001 from the Getúlio Vargas Foundation of Rio de Janeiro, was a Visiting Research Fellow in Law in 2008 at the Columbia University, New York, received a doctorate in law in 2010 from the Federal University of Rio Grande do Sul, took a specialism in European Law in 2014 at the University of Rome "Tor Vergata," and took a specialism in Law and Economics in 2018 at the University of Chicago Law School. Professor Battesini is the author of numerous articles and books, in particular the book *Law and Economics: New Horizons in the Study of Tort Law in Brazil*. He received the Robert D. Cooter–Microsoft prize in Law and Economics in 2010. Currently, he is *Adjunct Director of the School of Advocacy General of the Union*. – and he has been a Federal Attorney of the Advocacy General of the Union since 1992.

Magnum Koury de Figueiredo Eltz was born on September 6, 1985, in the city of Porto Alegre, Rio Grande do Sul, Brazil. He received a bachelor's degree in 2008 from Uniritter, an LLM in international and national environmental law in 2010 from the Federal University of Rio Grande do Sul, an LLM in law and economics in 2012 from the Federal University of Rio Grande do Sul and an MBA in Corporative Management in 2016 from the Brazilian Institute of Management and Business. In 2013, he was a Visiting Scholar at the Law and Economics Program at Berkeley Law. In 2017 he received the title of Master in Law by the Federal University of Rio Grande do Sul, and currently is a PhD applicant at the Federal University of Rio Grande do Sul and MBA in Financial and Tax Management applicant at the Brazilian Tax Faculty. He was

The Authors

the Academic Coordinator of LLM in Law and Economics of the Federal University of Rio Grande do Sul (2016–2017) and Coordinator of the Master in Business and Administration in Environmental Management at the Brazilian Institute of Management and Business (2016–2017). Currently, he is a Special Legal and Debureaucratization Assistant at the State of Rio Grande do Sul, Professor and Writer at Grupo A Publisher, and Researcher at the Rio Grande do Sul Bar Research Group in Law and Economics.

Cesar Santolim was born in the city of Santo Ângelo, Rio Grande do Sul, Brazil. He received a bachelor's degree in law in 1982 from the Federal University of Rio Grande do Sul, a bachelor's degree in economics in 1984 from the Federal University of Rio Grande do Sul, a master's in law in 1993 from the Federal University of Rio Grande do Sul, and a doctorate in law in 2004 from the Federal University of Rio Grande do Sul. He was Visiting Scholar and Adjunct Professor in Law in 2011 at the University of Illinois, and took a postdoctorate in law in 2014 at the University of Lisbon. Professor Santolim is the author of numerous articles and books. He was also a Public Attorney of the State of Rio Grande do Sul and an auditor (member) of the Court of Auditors of the State of Rio Grande do Sul. Currently, he is Titular Professor of Law at the Federal University of Rio Grande do Sul and a lawyer.

Table of Contents

Table of Contents

Table of Contents

List of Abbreviations

BRICS	Brazil, Russia, India, China, and South Africa
CDC	Consumer's Defense Code
DPVAT	Insurance for Automobile Vehicle Owners
STF	Federal Supreme Court (*Supremo Tribunal Federal*)
STJ	Superior Court of Justice (*Superior Tribunal de Justiça*)
SUS	Uniform Health System (*Sistema Único de Saúde*)
TJRS	Court of Justice of Rio Grande do Sul (*Tribunal de Justiça do Rio Grande do Sul*)
TST	Superior Court of Labor (*Tribunal Superior do Trabalho*)

List of Abbreviations

General Introduction

§1. THE GENERAL BACKGROUND OF THE COUNTRY

I. Geography

1. Based on total area, Brazil is the fifth largest country in the world, after Canada, Russia, China, and the USA. Brazil is located in the western hemisphere and is composed of 26 contiguous states, the Federal District of Brasilia, and 5,570 municipalities. Brazil consists of 8,515,767,049[1] sq. kms of land and water and shares land borders in the north with Venezuela, Guyana, Suriname, and the overseas territory of French Guiana; in the northwest with Colombia; in the west with Bolivia and Peru; in the southwest with Argentina and Paraguay; and in the south with Uruguay. Many island chains are considered as part of Brazilian territory, namely: Atol das Rocas, São Pedro, and São Paulo's Archipelago, Fernando de Noronha, Trindade and Martim Vaz. The capital of Brazil is Brasilia, Federal District, with a population of 2,852,372 (data from 2014). In June 2014, Brazil had a population of 202,768,562 inhabitants. The ethnic composition of Brazil is 47.51% Caucasian, 7.52% African American, 1% Asian, 0.42% Native American, with 43.42% being multiracial.[2] The main language spoken in Brazil is Portuguese, with about 237 extant Native American languages and small populations of Spanish, Italian, German, Dutch, Japanese, Arabic, and Korean speakers.[3]

2. Brazil's large territory comprises different ecosystems, such as the Amazon rainforest, recognized as having the greatest biological diversity in the world,[4] with the Atlantic Forest and the Cerrado, sustaining the greatest biodiversity.[5] In the south, the Araucaria pine forest grows under temperate conditions. The rich wildlife

---

1. Data acquired from IBGE – Brazilian Institute for Geographic and Economic Data (*Instituto Brasileiro de dados Geográficos e Econômicos*), available at http://www.ibge.gov.br/home/estatistica/.
2. Data from the 2010 IBGE's Census available at http://www.ibge.gov.br/home/estatistica/.
3. *See* ETHNOLOGUE, Languages of the World. Available at http://www.ethnologue.com/country/br and CENSUS, IBGE. Available at http://censo2010.ibge.gov.br/apps/atlas.
4. *See* MSN. ENCARTA. "Plant and Animal Life." Archived from the original on Oct. 31, 2009. Retrieved Jun. 12, 2008. San Francisco.
5. *See* MSN. ENCARTA. "Environmental Issues." Archived from the original on Oct. 31, 2009. Retrieved Jun. 12, 2008. San Francisco.

of Brazil reflects the variety of natural habitats. Scientists estimate that the total number of plant and animal species in Brazil could approach 4 million, mostly invertebrates.

3. As for animals native to Brazil, the jaguar is a typical wild animal, mainly found in the Amazon jungle. Larger mammals include carnivores such as pumas, jaguars, ocelots, rare bush dogs, and foxes, and herbivores such as peccaries, tapirs, anteaters, sloths, opossums, and armadillos. Deer are plentiful in the south, and many species of New World monkeys are found in the northern rainforests. Concern for the environment has grown in response to global interest in environmental issues.[6] Brazil's Amazon Basin is home to an extremely diverse array of fish species, including the red-bellied piranha. Despite its reputation as a ferocious freshftwater fish, the red-bellied piranha is actually a generally timid scavenger. Biodiversity can contribute to agriculture, livestock, forestry, and fish extraction. However, almost all economically exploited species of plants, such as soybeans and coffee, or animals, such as chickens, are imported from other countries, and the economic use of native species still stutters. In Brazilian GDP, the forest sector represents just over 1% and fishing 0.4%.

4. Brazil is also part of the Guarani Aquifer, located beneath the surface of Argentina, Brazil, Paraguay, and Uruguay, which is one of the world's largest aquifer systems and is an important source of fresh water. Named after the Guarani people, it covers 1,200,000 sq. kms (460,000 sq. miles), with a volume of about 40,000 cu km (9,600 cu mi), a thickness of between 50 m (160 ft) and 800 m (2,600 ft) and a maximum depth of about 1,800 me (5,900 ft). It is estimated to contain about 37,000 cu km (8,900 cu mi) of water (arguably the largest single body of groundwater in the world, although the overall volume of the constituent parts of the Great Artesian Basin is much larger), with a total recharge rate of about 166 km^3/year from precipitation.[7]

5. In the international economic sphere, Brazil is part of the Southern Common Market, which is a regional integration process, originally instituted by Argentina, Brazil, Paraguay, and Uruguay, and later incorporating Venezuela and Bolivia (in the process of acceding). The goals of this South American trade agreement are to create a common ground for trade opportunities and investments focused on international markets. It is implemented by multiple bilateral agreements and annual

---

6. *See Ibid.*

7. *See* GOMES et al. *Revista do Departamento de Geografia,* 18 (2006) 67–74. *"CLASSIFICAÇÃO DAS ÁREAS DE RECARGA DO SISTEMA AQÜÍFERO GUARANI NO BRASIL EM DOMÍNIOS PEDOMORFOAGROCLIMÁTICOS – SUBSÍDIO AOS ESTUDOS DE AVALIAÇÃO DE RISCO DE CONTAMINAÇÃO DAS ÁGUAS SUBTERRÂNEAS." CLASSIFICAÇÃO DAS ÁREAS DE RECARGA DO SISTEMA AQÜÍFERO GUARANI NO BRASIL EM DOMÍNIOS PEDOMORFOA-GROCLIMÁTICOS – SUBSÍDIO AOS ESTUDOS DE AVALIAÇÃO DE RISCO DE CONTAMI-NAÇÃO DAS ÁGUAS* (n.d.): n. pag. October 2005. Available at https://www.embrapa.br/busca-de-publicacoes/-/publicacao/15909/classificacao-das-areas-de-recarga-do-sistema-aquifero-guarani-no-brasil-em-dominios-pedomorfoagroclimaticos---subsidios-aos-estudos-de-avaliacao-do-risco-de-contaminacao-das-aguas-subterraneas.

meetings. The potential of Mercosur, according to the organization itself, lies in its territory of almost 15 million km², its great variety of wealth and natural resources, and a population of 295 million.[8]

6. Brazil is also part of the economic trade organization known as BRICS. BRICS is the acronym for an association of five major emerging national economies: Brazil, Russia, India, China, and South Africa. The grouping was originally known as "BRIC" before the inclusion of South Africa in 2010. The BRICS members are all developing or newly industrialized countries, but they are distinguished by their large, fast-growing economies and their significant influence on regional and global affairs; all five are G-20 members. Since 2009, the BRICS nations have met annually at formal summits. Russia currently holds the chair of the BRICS group and hosted the group's seventh summit in July 2015.

7. As of 2015, the five BRICS countries represent over 3 billion people or 42% of the world's population; all five members are in the top twenty-five of the world by population, and four are in the top ten. The five nations have a combined nominal GDP of USD 16.039 trillion, equivalent to approximately 20% of gross world product, and an estimated USD 4 trillion in combined foreign reserves. The BRICS have received both praise and criticism from numerous commentators. Bilateral relations among BRICS nations have mainly been conducted on the basis of non-interference, equality, and mutual benefit (win-win).[9]

II. History

8. The origins of Brazil as an independent state are recent. The discovery of its territory is attributed to the Portuguese explorer Pedro Alverez Cabral in 1500,[10] although indications of the first human activity on Brazilian territory go back as far as 60,000 years.[11] Most academics agree that there were people living in the Americas who originated from Asia and Europe prior to its discovery by the Europeans and who would be referred to as "Indians" when the explorations of the 1400s and 1500s took place in the course of exploring new routes to Asia.[12]

9. In 1534, the Portuguese king D. João III had divided the colonial territory defined by the Tordesilhas Treaty of 1494[13] with Spain into twelve Hereditary Capitanies, controlled by selected families. In 1549, the control system was considered

---

8. *See* MERCOSUR. *"En pocas palabras."* Montevideo. Visited in 2016. Available at www.mercosur-.int.
9. *See* GUTTENBERG, The Sino-Brazilian Principles in a Latin American and BRICS Context: The Case for Comparative Public Budgeting Legal Research. Wisconsin International Law Journal. May 13, 2015. Retrieved Jun. 6, 2015.
10. *See* BOXER, *IMPÉRIO MARÍTIMO PORTUGUÊS* – 1415–1825, 2011, São Paulo.
11. *See* CUNHA, *História dos Índios no Brasil*, 1992, São Paulo.
12. *See* BRAD SHAW FOUNDATION, "Journey of mankind." Retrieved Nov. 17, 2015 Available at http://www.bradshawfoundation.com/stephenoppenheimer/index.php.
13. *See* BOXER, *IMPÉRIO MARÍTIMO PORTUGUÊS* – 1415–182, 2011, São Paulo.

flawed and was extended by the king when he nominated a general-governor for the whole territory.[14] The Portuguese assimilated some native tribes as their own, while others remained enslaved or were killed by European diseases. Only in the sixteenth century were Africans brought as slaves to Brazil to aid sugarcane production, the first crop production cycle in Brazil.[15] During this period, the Portuguese had ignored the existence of the Tordesilhas Treaty and expanded their territory by the initiative called "Bandeiras,"[16] which led to several wars in the sixteenth and seventeenth centuries with other European countries such as France in the north, the Netherlands in the northeast, and Spain in the south. By the end of the seventeenth century, the search for gold[17] had inspired a new expansion called the "Bandeirantes" initiative, which led to the Emboabas war between new and old Portuguese colonizers. To guarantee order, the crown ordered the crushing of all rebellions such as the Quilombo dos Palmares[18] (rebellion of black slaves) or the Inconfidência Mineira (a separatist movement).

10. At the end of the year 1807,[19] Napoleonic forces had entered Portugal, forcing Prince D. João VI to move the crown from Lisbon to Brazil.[20] The arrival of the Portuguese court brought Brazil its first institutions such as a financial market, a national bank, and the end of the monopoly of Portugal on Brazilian imports.[21] In retaliation for his auto-exile, the Portuguese prince brought about the conquest of French Guiana.[22] With the end of the Peninsular War in Europe, Portugal sought the return of the royal family, but it was not their intention to go back to Portugal.[23] Thus, the United Kingdom of Brazil and the Algarves were created, but the Pernambucan Independence Revolution in 1817 and the Porto Revolution in 1820 were unpleasant surprises for both the Portuguese and the Brazilians. In 1821 D. João VI returned to Portugal and left his son Pedro I as Prince Regent of the Kingdom of Brazil.[24]

11. Portugal tried to force Brazil back to the status of a colonial state in 1815, a move which was resisted by both the Brazilians and Prince D. Pedro I, who declared the independence of Brazil from Portugal on September 7, 1822.[25] On December 1, 1822, the Brazilian Empire was created, but only in 1825 was its status recognized

---

14. *Ibid.*
15. *Ibid.*
16. *See* HERNANI, *Dicionário das Batalhas Brasileiras*, 1996, São Paulo.
17. *See* HOLANDA, CAMPOS & FAUSTO, *Boris História geral da civilização brasileira*, 1963, São Paulo.
18. *Supra.*
19. *See* MELLO, *Forças Militares no Brasil Colonial*, Rio de Janeiro, at 51, 59, 85. Available at http://www.e-papers.com.br/produtos.asp?codigo_produto=1667.
20. *See* BOXER, *IMPÉRIO MARÍTIMO PORTUGUÊS* – 1415–1825, 2011, São Paulo.
21. *See* BARCELLOS & AZEVEDO, *Histórias do Mercado de Capitais no Brasil.* Introduction by Ney Carvalho, at Xiv, 2011, São Paulo.
22. *See* BUENO, *Brasil Uma História*, 2004, São Paulo.
23. *See* MOSHER, Political Struggle, Ideology, and State Building: Pernambuco and the Construction of Brazil, 1817–1850. 2008 [S.l.]: University of Nebraska Press. Lincoln.
24. *See* LUSTOSA, *D. Pedro I – um herói sem nenhum caráter*, 2006, São Paulo.
25. *See* VIANNA, *História do Brasil: período colonial, monarquia e república*, 1994, São Paulo.

as independent of Portugal.[26] Brazil's first Constitution was promulgated in 1824 and accepted by all the municipalities of the country. In order to keep the crown in his family, Pedro I went back to Portugal in 1831 and left to his son Pedro II the title of Prince Regent. During this period several revolutions took place, such as the Cabanagem in the north, the Malês and Sabinada in the northeast, and the Farroupilha in the south.[27] In the middle of this turmoil, D. Pedro II was nominated Emperor to calm the masses in 1840.[28]

12. After losing the province of Cisplatin, which became Uruguay, Brazil won three wars, the War of the River Plate, the Uruguay War, and the Paraguay War. In 1850,[29] due to economic pressure and the advent of the Aberdeen Bill, Brazil ended slavery in its territory. In 1889, with the country weakened by economic stagnation and clashes between the rural and financial oligarchies, the Brazilian army staged a *coup d'état*, which ushered Brazil into the Republican Era.[30] In 1891, a new Constitution was promulgated, making the Republic of Brazil official, although only in 1894 would direct elections be held (with voting only by certain male citizens).[31]

13. At the beginning of the republican period, Brazil had a neutral international position, until the Acrian episode[32] that led to Brazilian participation in World War I.[33] Between 1891 and 1920, internal struggles led to the 1930 revolution that culminated with the defeat of the military occupation and the rise of President Getúlio Vargas,[34] who began his regime as a dictator under a state of emergency and was embroiled in struggles with the São Paulo oligarchies (1932) and the communists (1935).[35] In 1938, a new struggle emerged between Vargas and the Integrality Movement (the Brazilian Fascist Party). Brazil was considered neutral in World War II[36] until an attack on Brazilian ships in 1942, which led to Brazil sending forces to help the allies in Europe in 1944. After the end of World War II, the forces that Vargas had sent to Europe came back and instigated a new *coup d'état* to oust him.[37]

---

26. *Supra.*
27. *See* PRADO, *A Formação das Nações Latino-Americanas; Capítulo 5. O regime monárquico e o estado nacional,* 1986, Campinas, at 61 and following.
28. *See* FAUSTO, *História do Brasil,* 2012, São Paulo.
29. *See* LYRA, *História de Dom Pedro II* (1825–1891): Ascenção (1825–1870) (in Portuguese) 1, 1977, Belo Horizonte; LYRA, *História de Dom Pedro II (1825–1891): Fastígio (1870–1880)* (in Portuguese) 2, 1977, Belo Horizonte; LYRA, *História de Dom Pedro II (1825–1891): Declínio* (1880–1891) (in Portuguese) 3, 1977, Belo Horizonte.
30. *See* PENNA, *O progresso da ordem: O florianismo e a construção da República,* 2008, Rio de Janeiro, at 59.
31. *See* LEAL, *Coronelismo, Enxada e Voto: o município e o sistema representativo no Brasil,* 1949, São Paulo.
32. *See* RODRIGUEZ, José Honório & Ricardo A.S. Seitenfus. Leda Boechat Rodrigues, *História Diplomática do Brasil,* 1995, São Paulo.
33. *See* BARBOSA, *A raiz das coisas: o Brasil no mundo, Civilização Brasileira,* 2008, São Paulo.
34. *See* AGGIO, *Política e sociedade no Brasil,* 1930–1964, Annablume, 2002, São Paulo.
35. *See* FAUSTO, *História do Brasil,* 2012, São Paulo.
36. *See* SEITENFUS, "2.2," *A entrada do Brasil na Segunda Guerra Mundial,* 2000 Porto Alegre, at 116–168.
37. *Supra.*

14. In 1946, democracy was restored with the election of Eurico Gaspar Dutra as president. Reelected in 1950, Vargas tragically committed suicide after an intense political crisis.[38] In 1955, Juscelino Kubitschek was elected. His conciliatory attitude towards political opponents helped to keep his government free of major crises and to improve the performance of the economic and industrial sectors. His main achievement as president was the building of Brasilia, the new capital of the country.[39] His successor was Jânio Quadros, who renounced the presidential role in 1961, leaving the position to his vice-president João Goulart who was deposed by a military coup in 1964 due to his left-wing tendencies.

15. The new regime was supposed to be transitional, but would end only in 1985.[40] The military dictatorship in Brazil was marked by violence, censorship, and the repression and torture of left-wing politicians and students, although the period was also known as the "economic miracle" of the 1970s and led to economic prosperity. Under pressure from many left-wing rebellions, the regime passed an Amnesty Act in 1979 and after the advent of the movement "Diretas Já" (direct vote now), a new democracy was born in 1985.[41]

16. Tancredo Neves was the first elected president, but due to severe medical problems, he did not take up his position, ceding to his vice-president José Sarney the role of the first democratic president of Brazil after the military period. Many economic crises and monetary issues led to the election of the brand new candidate Fernando Collor de Mello[42] in 1989; he was deposed in 1992 by the first impeachment for financial scandal in the history of Brazil. The role of president was then filled by the vice-president Itamar Franco who was known, along with Minister Fernando Henrique Cardoso, for the implementation of the successful Real Economic Plan, which introduced the Real currency, still used to this date. The new plan led to Fernando Henrique Cardoso's election in 1994, and marked new economic stability in Brazil and the beginning of the privatization process in many state companies in fields such as communications, electricity, and mineral exploration.[43]

17. The success of Cardoso's first mandate led to his reelection in 1998, but his second mandate was marred by increasing social inequality, which led to the election of Luiz Inácio Lula da Silva in 2002. He had a left-wing agenda and started many social programs in Brazil, implementing public scholarships for private education, basic food aid for students and their families, and a large-scale housing program. His popularity guaranteed his reelection in 2006 and made for a clean sweep in the election of his political successor Dilma Rousseff, the first woman elected as

---

38. *See* BUENO, *Brasil uma História*, 2004, São Paulo.
39. *See* SKIDMORE, *História Geral*, 2003, Recife.
40. *See* GASPARI, *A ditadura escancarada*, 2002, São Paulo.
41. *See* MENDONÇA, Daniel, *Tancredo Neves – Da Distensão à Nova República*, 2004, Santa Cruz do Sul.
42. *See* PAIVA, *Era outra história: política social do governo Itamar Franco, 1992–1994*, 2009, Juiz de Fora.
43. *See* FAUSTO and DEVOTO, *História do Brasil*, 2004. São Paulo.

the president of Brazil in 2010.[44] Her first mandate has shown the impact on the economy of the many social projects initiated by her party, which led to protests in 2013 under the flag of the reduction of transport fees;[45] however, the social aid was sufficient to guarantee her reelection in 2014 on a platform promising new economic reforms and maintaining the social programs previously implemented. The second Rousseff government would be hard on the presidency, as many protests, in addition to the growing economic crisis, led to the controversial impeachment process initiated by the Chamber of Deputies at the end of 2015.[46] As a result of corruption scandals exposed by the media and the federal courts, the largest protest in the history of Brazil has reinforced the popular call for the president's dismissal.[47] On April 17, 2016, the Chamber of Deputies voted for Rousseff's dismissal,[48] leading to the historic defeat of the Senate and the legal provisional dismissal of the president for 180 days until the definitive vote of the Senate, due in September 2016.[49] Meanwhile, vice-president Michel Temer is the new president of Brazil, representing a shift of political standards, from a long-standing left-wing government, started by Luis Inácio Lula da Silva, to a right-wing government led by the PMDB party. In the following presidential election, in 2018, Jair Messias Bolsonaro has become the first military president elected since the military regime. During the first year of his mandate, the president along with the Ministry of Economy, Paulo Guedes, led a liberal reform on the Brazilian economy which has been halted in a radical shift of approach caused by the COVID-19 pandemic starting in 2020. Currently, COVID-19 has reached a death toll of 500,000 persons, within one year and three months. The contamination has reached 10 million of Brazilians and impacted 4.3% of the GNP in 2020.[50]

III. Political System

18. The Federal Constitution of Brazil, states in its First Article that:

---

44. *See* UOL, *"Jornais Internacionais destacam a vitória de Dilma."* http://eleicoes.uol.com.br/2010/ultimas-noticias/2010/10/31/jornais-internacionais-destacam-a-vitoria-de-dilma.jhtm.
45. *See* PORTAL TERRA, *Governo brasileiro é pressionado por históricos protestos.* Visited in Jun. 25, 2013. Available at http://noticias.terra.com.br/brasil/governo-brasileiro-e-pressionado-por-historicos-protestos,f614e49fccf5f310VgnCLD2000000ec6eb0aRCRD.html.
46. *See* FOLHA, *"Cunha deflagra processo de impechment contra Dilma."* Available at http://www1.folha.uol.com.br/poder/2015/12/1714133-cunha-deflara-processo-de-impeachment-contra-dlma.shtml.
47. *See* G1. *"Manifestações contra o Governo Dilma ocorrem pelo País."* Available at http://g1.globo.com/politica/noticia/2016/03/manifestacoes-contra-governo-dilma-ocorrem-pelo-pais.html.
48. TERRA, *"Derrota na Câmara deixa governo Dilma mais perto do fim."* Available at http://noticias.terra.com.br/brasil/derrota-na-camara-deixa-governo-dilma-mais-perto-do-fim,10cf69a55c005088ab079943bfe785a4qa8lwiak.html.
49. GLOBO, *"Processo de Impeachment é aberto e Dilma é afastada por até 180 dias."* Available at http://g1.globo.com/politica/processo-de-impeachment-de-dilma/noticia/2016/05/processo-de-impeachment-e-aberto-e-dilma-e-afastada-por-ate-180-dias.html.
50. *See, Economia na Pandemia.* Available at: https://valor.globo.com/coronavirus/a-economia-na-pandemia/. Also, *Brasil atinge a marca de 500 mil mortes pela Covid.* Available at: https://g1.globo.com/jornal-nacional/noticia/2021/06/19/brasil-atinge-marca-tragica-de-500-mil-mortes-pela-covid.ghtml.

the Federal Republic of Brazil is formed by the insoluble union of the Federated States and Municipalities and the Federal District and it is constituted as a Democratic State of Law founded on Sovereignty, Citizenship, the Dignity of the Human Person, the Social Values of Work and Free Initiative, and Political Pluralism.[51]

19. Brazil is a federal republic, represented by the union of twenty-six contiguous states and the Federal District of Brasilia. The political system is presidential, with democratic representation. The power within the Union is represented by the president who is the Head of State and represents Brazil diplomatically. The states are considered to have autonomy guaranteed by the Constitution and have the power to make their own constitutions, as they are considered independent municipalities, with the power to promulgate their own laws and guidelines.

20. The roles of Head of State and Head of Government are attributed to the president of the Republic. The republican system in Brazil guarantees that the president is elected by direct, universal, and obligatory vote for a limited period, remaining in power for only two consecutive mandates. Finally, the democratic regime gives the people the power to elect the president, the members of parliament, and to directly influence Brazilian politics through plebiscites, referendums, and popular initiatives.

21. According to the *Economist* Democracy Index, Brazil, which had at the time of the first edition of this chapter a high performance on electoral pluralism (9.5) and civil liberties (9.1),[52] and had above average government functionality (7.5), although it had an inferior performance in political participation (5.0) and culture (4.3), according to 2012 data,[53] remains a "flawed democracy" according to the same index in 2020 numbers, although it has reached a better electoral process and pluralism (9.58), and political participation (6.11) and culture (5.63), the government functionality has dropped to (5.36), as well as civil liberties, which are now at (7.94).[54]

22. Article 2 of the Federal Constitution states that the powers of the Union are supplementary and independent of each other and comprise the legislature, the executive, and the judiciary. The executive Head of State is the president of the Republic, elected by direct vote for a four-year mandate, which can be extended for four more years through reelection. In the federated states, the executive is represented by governors and in the municipalities by mayors. Legislative powers are concentrated in the Union by the National Congress, which is bicameral, divided into the Chamber of Deputies (representing the people's interests) and the Senate

51. *See* BRASIL, Constituição Federal de 1988, Brazilian Congress – 1988. Available at http://www.planalto.gov.br/ccivil_03/Constituicao/Constituicao.htm.
52. *See* THE ECONOMIST. Democracy Index Economist Intelligence Unit. 2010. Visited in Jun. 21, 2013. Available at http://www.eiu.com/home.aspx#introduction.
53. *Ibid.* 2012
54. THE ECONOMIST. Democracy Index 2020: In Sickness and in Health?. Available at: EIU.com. Retrieved February 2, 2021.

(representing the states' interests) for a mandate of four years. The Chamber of Deputies is comprised of a proportional ratio of representatives according to the state's population, as the Senate is comprised of three senators for each state, who have a mandate of eight years. In the federated states, the legislature is represented by the state assemblies and in the municipalities by the county chambers.[55] Finally, different courts in Brazil represent the judiciary. In the federated states, it is composed of state courts formed by local forums of primary judges and state courts formed by groups of senior judges; in the Union, by the federal justice and federal courts and at the High Court level by the Superior Justice Court and the Supreme Federal Court, together with labor justice represented by labor judges, regional courts, and the Superior Labor Court. Judges are not elected in Brazil: they are chosen by public selection based on their legal careers and performance on tests in the case of lower courts and by nomination by their peers in state, federal, and labor courts and by the executive in the higher courts.

23. Article 3 of the Constitution states that the fundamental objectives of the Republic are to build a free, just, and fraternal society; to guarantee national development; to eradicate poverty and marginalization, and to reduce social and regional inequality; and to promote the welfare of all, without prejudice against origin, race, gender, color, age, or any discrimination.

24. As for international relations, Brazil states the following principles in Article 4: national independence, the primacy of human rights, the self-determination of nations, non-intervention, state equity, peaceful defense, pacific conflict solution, rejection of terrorism and racism, cooperation between nations for the progress of humankind, and political asylum concession. In addition, the same paragraph indicates that Brazil will seek the economic, political, social, and cultural integration of the nations of Latin America, aiming to achieve a Latin American community of nations.

IV. Economic and Social Values

25. Brazil is a country that still depends mostly on the wealth generated by its agriculture and meat production sectors, though it has nascent activities in both the manufacturing and services sectors. Historically, the economy of Brazil started mostly with the extraction of its natural wealth through the exporting of wood, gold, and rubber to Portugal as part of the Colonial Pact. As Brazil became an empire of its own, the industry was still lacking, as the oligarchies became the main source of wealth, exporting milk and coffee worldwide. During his second reign, Pedro II brought innovations such as the train and the telegraph to Brazil, starting a fever of novelties and an urge for industrialization, but it was only after the revolution of the 1930s that Getúlio Vargas would invest in Brazilian industry, which reached its peak during the military dictatorship, particularly during the 1970s. Today, the Brazilian

---

55. Adapted from the text of WIKIPEDIA, The Free Encyclopedia. Available at: http://pt.wikipedia.org /wiki/Pol%C3%ADtica_do_Brasil.

economy is still agro-based; although some efforts to innovate are being made, the institutions of the country are still struggling to get the industry established.[56]

26.   Current Brazilian economic and social values can be found in the Brazilian Federal Constitution, which states in its Article 170, the "general principles of economic activity," in Article 193 the guidelines of the "Social Order," and in a spread of articles the principles of taxation, the health care system, and social aid.[57]

27.   Article 170 states as the general principles of economic activity:

> national sovereignty, private ownership, the social function of property, the free market, consumer protection, the protection of the environment and differential treatment according to the impact of production and services and their production processes; the reduction of regional and social inequality; the search for full employment; and special treatment for small corporations with their residence and administration in the country.

Its text states that "the free exercise of any economic activity is secured for all, independently of public authorization, except in cases set out in law."

28.   In addition, Article 5, which sets out the fundamental rights of Brazil (not revocable by constitutional amendment), guarantees the general principles of:

> equality, liberty, security and property, adding to: the freedom of speech, privacy, inviolability of private property (except in flagrant disasters to give aid or by legal order during the day); mail security; the free exercise of work, a craft or profession under the terms of the law; free access to information; free movement within the national territory during times of peace; freedom of reunion; the freedom of association (except for paramilitary purposes); the social function of property; the protection of private property and compensation for public expropriation; the payment of damages for the public use of private property; the protection of small rural areas for debit payment purposes; the protection of authors' rights, and of intellectual property; the right of inheritance; the defense of the consumer; and finally, the rule of law.

29.   In the agribusiness sector, Article 184 states that "Agriculture and Meat production must accomplish their social function; otherwise, the government will expropriate the land to fulfil this function defined by law." This article shows not only that land distribution of Brazil is a concern of the government, but also that private property is not fully protected for all uses by its proprietors. This endorses the goals of the Brazilian government to generate employment and optimally use the country's land. On the other hand, the empty concept of "social function" fails

---

56. *See* FILIPPI, *Evolução econômica e institucional do setor primário no Brasil: em direção ao desenvolvimento rural?*, 2006, Maputo.
57. *See* BRASIL, *Constituição Federal de 1988*. Available at http://www.planalto.gov.br/ccivil_03/Constituicao/Constituicao.htm.

to protect producers, who can be deprived of their lands by the administration giving its own interpretation of "social function."

30. The financial market in Brazil is a complex phenomenon. It started with the royal family from Portugal fleeing to Brazil and opening the first Bank of Brazil, which went bankrupt during the First Reign, and led to the opening of the second Bank of Brazil from the former "Bank Mauá" and the opening up of the financial market during the 1990s to foreign banks. Today Brazil has many big banks, though smaller banks are responsible for the main financial operations, called "microcredit" investments to fulfill the market needs of the "new middle class" promoted by the Luiz Inácio Lula da Silva and Dilma Rousseff governments. The Constitution of Brazil defines in Article 192 that the national financial system is structured to promote the balanced development of the country and to serve collective interests, including those of credit cooperatives. Though the financial market has been responsible for Brazilian development in recent years due to the rise of the new middle class, many struggles are taking place due to the ultra-bankruptcy of the same new middle class, which has led to protests about the direction the Brazilian economy is taking during the second mandate of Dilma Rousseff.

31. Title VIII of the Brazilian Constitution deals with social order and in its Article 193 states, "the social order has its base in work and its goal is welfare and social justice." Article 194 defines social security as an integrated action package provided by society and the state with the aim of securing rights to health care, retirement, and social assistance. The text of Article 194 highlights the following principles for this purpose: universal coverage of services; uniformity and equivalence of benefits and services between rural and urban populations; selectivity and distribution of benefits and services; prohibition of reduction of labor benefits; EQUITY in the distribution of costs; diversity in the financial base; the democratic character and decentralization of the administration through quasi-management with the participation of workers, employers, the retired, and the government in plural offices.

32. In section II of this chapter, Article 196 establishes that the health care system is a right of everyone and a duty of the state, granted through social and economic policies aiming to reduce the risks of sickness and other illnesses and offering universal and equal access to actions and services to protect, promote, and recover health. The Uniform Health System (*Sistema Único de Saúde* – SUS) is defined in Article 198 as a region-wide network constituted according to the following principles: decentralization, with a single director in each state division; integrated service, with priority for preventive action; and finally, community participation.

33. Article 201 establishes the public security system, which is organized under a central regime with a contributory character and mandatory affiliation, observing criteria that preserve financial and actuarial equilibria. It covers: events of sickness, handicap, death, and aging; protection for mothers, especially during pregnancy;

protection for workers and those unintentionally unemployed; family salary and financial aid for the dependents of those on low income; death pensions for companions and dependents.

34. Section IV established the social care system which is extended to anyone who needs it, regardless of whether they have paid social security contributions or not. It aims to protect the institution of the family, motherhood, childhood, young people, and the elderly; to help children and teenagers in need; to promote integration into the work market; to habilitate and rehabilitate people with disabilities and to re-introduce them into their communities; and finally, to guarantee a minimum wage to anyone who has a disability and to elderly people who are proved not to have the means to sustain themselves or do not have such support from their families.

35. Chapter 2 of the Brazilian Constitution indicates the social rights to be protected by the state. In its Article 6 are stated the social rights of education, health care, sustenance, work, housing, leisure, security, social security, protection of mothers and children, and assistance for those in need.

36. Article 7 defines the rights of the urban and rural workers to sustain their social condition in the face of arbitrary or unjust dismissal, which will require compensatory damages and other rights defined by law such as unemployment insurance, a warranty fund by the length of service. A minimum wage is established by law that is capable of meeting vital and basic needs such as family housing, and sustenance; education; health; leisure; clothing; hygiene; transportation; and social security with periodic adjustments to preserve its buying power.

The minimum wage varies according to the hours and complexity of work. Wages cannot be reduced, except through class agreements and wages below the legal minimum are prohibited. The one-third of the minimum wage concept is based on full remuneration or the retirement wage; night-time wages are higher than daytime wages; there is a legal punishment for withholding wages; participation in profits or results is not dependent on remuneration and may exceptionally include participation in corporate management as defined by law; a family wage is paid to dependents with low income by law; work journeys cannot be contracted for more than eight hours a day and forty-four hours a week, although compensation for hours is possible through class agreements; a journey of six hours is the maximum, unless negotiated in class agreements; paid weekly days off must be given, preferably on Sundays. Overtime wages should be 50% higher than the regular wage; annual vacations should be given with at least one-third of regular wages in addition to the salary for the period; maternity leave is allowed for 120 days without a change of wage and working status; paternity leave is on the terms given by law. Women are protected in the work market by specific incentives in the terms given by law. In addition, the following measures are mandated:

– prior notice proportional to the time of service, with a fixed minimum of thirty days;
– reduction of the risks related to work, through health, hygiene and security laws;

- additional wages for hazardous, dangerous or unhealthy activities;
- early retirement;
- free assistance to children and dependents from birth up to five years of age in kindergarten and pre-schools;
- recognition of conventions and collective bargaining at work (collective contracts are the only way to negotiate contractual labor clauses in Brazil);
- protection from the automatization process;
- work liability insurance paid by the employer not excluding damages due to negligence or intention;
- the possibility of legal actions to claim working related credits with a limitation period of five years for urban and rural workers after two years from the end of the working contract;
- prohibition of salary discrimination according to sex, age, color or civil status;
- prohibition of any discrimination of salary and admission criteria for handicapped persons;
- prohibition of any differentiation between manual, technical, and intellectual works and workers;
- prohibition of night shifts, dangerous, or unhealthy works for workers below the age of 18 or any night shifts for workers under the age of 16, except for apprentices of at least 14 years;
- equal rights for workers and eventual servants (those with less than three months of labor). The paragraph adds that domestic workers (namely, cleaning workers and housekeepers) have the same rights, social security access and a simplified tax system so that they may become more equally treated, as follows. The paragraph adds that:

> domestic workers have the same rights set out in IV, VI, VII, VIII, X, XIII, XV, XVI, XVII, XVIII, XIX, XXI, XXII, XXIV, XXVI, XXX, XXXI and XXXIII and simplification of tax obligations set out in I, II, III, IX, XII, XXV and XXVIII, as integration into the social security system.

37. Article 8, in turn, states that professional and syndicate association is free, observing that the law cannot require state authorization for the foundation of a syndicate, except for the need to register with the competent agency, and is forbidden for the state to interfere in the syndicate's organization. More than one syndicate for an economic or professional category in the same territory is forbidden; the territory is defined by the workers and employers concerned, with the minimum territory being a county. The syndicate will promote the defense of collective and individual rights of the category in legal and administrative matters; the main assembly will state the contribution which will be paid at source to sustain the syndicate's representation, independent of the contribution stated by law. No one is obligated to join or to remain part of a syndicate. The participation of syndicates in collective negotiations at work is mandatory. Retired workers have the right to vote or to be voted on to syndicate organizations. It is forbidden to terminate the employment of a worker who is part of a syndicate from the time of the application to direct or represent the syndicate to one year after the mandate has finished, unless the

employee commits a severe fault according to the law. The text of this article states that its content also applies to rural syndicates and fishing organizations.

38.   Article 9 secures the right to strike to defend workers' interests, except for those working in essential activities or cases of abusive behavior. In addition, Article 10 secures the participation of workers and employers in public branches that are related to their professional and other interests. Finally, Article 11 states that in corporations with more than 200 employees elections are to be held for one representative to carry out direct negotiations with the employer.

39.   In order to sustain the state and its social security system, Brazil has a list of taxes and fees provided by the Constitution and defined by law. Article 153 states that Union taxes will cover: the importation of foreign products; the exportation of national or nationalized products; income of any nature; manufactured products; credit, exchange, and insurance related to credit titles and securities; rural property; great wealth in the terms of complementary law. For the federated states, Article 155 defines their taxes to cover the transfer through death and donation of any wealth or rights; operations related to the circulation of goods and transportation services between states and municipalities and communication, even though their origin is traced to foreign countries; and vehicles. Finally, Article 156 establishes that the municipalities can collect taxes based on: urban property; the transmission between living persons of any title by a trading act of real estate, except for warranties and the cessation of powers for their acquisition. The Constitution adds to the receipts of the federated states the restitution of taxes given to the Union by the autarchies and foundations (direct public administration branches) maintained by them and 20% of the taxes acquired by the Union, as mentioned in Article 154, I. As for the municipalities, Article 158 adds to their receipts the product of their collection of income taxes from the autarchies and foundations they maintain. The taxes, as revenue acquisition, are given by the executive power through the plurennial plan, budget directions and the annual budget that is reviewed by Congress according to Article 165 and the text of the Constitution.

§2.   Legal Systems

I.   Primacy of Legislation and Codification

40.   Brazilian law is considered to be a civil law legal system in the Roman-German tradition, as opposed to a common law system, where the rules are the consequence of tradition, customs, and jurisprudence, with only a few legal statements. Civil law works through law-making processes stemming directly from social customs to legislation which dictates current norms through extensive codification in the federal Constitution, federal laws, state laws, and municipality laws. According to Canotilho "the Brazilian Constitution was able to rise to the role of fundamental

legal rule."[58] In fact, "the Bill of 1988 is what might be called an analytical and overloaded constitution."[59] So a large number of issues that are not normally found in constitutional texts are present in the Brazilian Constitution, including some aspects of liability, and torts (e.g., public liability, Article 37, §6; judicial liability, Article 5, LXXV; employers' liability, Article 7, XXVIII; liability for radioactive damage, Article 21, XXIII, "c;" environmental damages, Article 225, §3; moral damages, Article 5, V e X). In addition, the Constitution is the supreme law in Brazil, and supersedes all and any other rules, whether statutory or not.

41. Regarding private law, its competence is usually federal. Private law and commercial law are usually regulated under federal laws, though both federal and state laws regulate consumer law, even though its guidelines are given by the Union. Historically, Brazil had a Commercial Code in 1850 and a Civil Code in 1916, but in 1990 the Consumer's Protection Code entered into force and in 2002 a new Civil Code was promulgated (which revoked both the Civil Code of 1916 and most of the 1850 Commercial Code). The Civil Code of 2002 (Law no. 10,406/2002) promoted the unification of the civil and commercial obligations, introduce the concept of "enterprise" as a substitute for the concept of "tradesman," modified contract law, property law and, mainly, tort law ("civil liability"). This Code is the main legal structure of the private law system in Brazil. The change is reinforced by the fact that it uses, in many circumstances, "open rules:" rules with abstract content, where the judge, case by case, must define the law. Together with other elements (constitutional change, use of principles, judicial activism), the "new" code implies important modifications to the private law scenario.

42. The Civil Code is divided into a general part and a special part. The general part is very important, as its concepts are necessary to civil law, because of its systematic structure, in contrast to the practical and jurisprudential character of common law. The special part is divided into the law of obligations (contracts and torts), enterprise law, property law, family law, and inheritance law. The Civil Code has 2046 articles: the first 232 are in the general part, and the others are in the special part, but the last 49 are final and transitional articles.

43. In the general part can be found rules about "persons," "things," "facts (that matter to the law)," "lawful and unlawful acts," "prescription (statute of limitations)" and "proof." The "law of obligation" has a "classification," and then rules about "transmission," "extinction (including payment)," "nonpayment," "contracts," "unilateral acts," "credit titles" and "civil liability." "Enterprise law" defines "entrepreneur," "corporation," "business unit," register, name, executive board, and other supplementary concepts. Property law is, basically, about "possession" and "property/ownership," but there are other rights about assets ("rights *in rem*"): surface, servitude, usufruct, use, habitation, rights of the promisor buyer of real estate,

---

58. *See* CANOTILHO, MENDES, SARLET, & STRECK (Coord.), *Comentários à Constituição do Brasil*, 2013, São Paulo, at 45.
59. *See* COELHO, in CANOTILHO, MENDES, SARLET, and STRECK, Lenio (Coord.), *Comentários à Constituição do Brasil*, 2013, São Paulo, at 62.

pledge, mortgage and "antichresis" (a Roman law pledge instrument). Family law has rules about personal rights (including marriage) and patrimonial rights, including rules about stable unions, tutelage and guardianship. Finally, inheritance law governs succession in general (legitimate succession, including necessary heirs, testate succession, and asset division).

44. It is fundamental to recognize that the Brazilian legal system has "microsystems." In addition to the main structure (the Civil Code), there are other legal structures, with one or more specific Acts which form these "microsystems." There is no necessary formal hierarchy between the Civil Code and the Acts that constitute these microsystems. Legal textbooks state that there is a "source dialogue" between the Civil Code and the Acts because there is a reciprocal influence. The main "microsystems," in private law, are "minors' law," "consumer law," "corporate law," "capital market law" and "credit titles law."

45. The Consumer Law (Law no. 8,078/90) has rules about consumer rights, criminal sanctions (in consumer relations), procedural issues (judicial), and a national system of consumer protection. Consumer rights consist of "general rules," "national consumer policies," "basic consumer rights," "product and services quality (prevention and liability)," "commercial practices," "contractual protection," "administrative sanctions" (applied by government agencies), "product and service quality," "health and security protection," "liability for the product/service," "liability for malfunction of the product/service," "prescription" (statute of limitations), and "disregard of legal entity." The "commercial practices" rules deal with the "offer," "publicity," "abusive practices," "debt charge" and "data banks." "Contractual protection" deals with "abusive clauses" and "adhesion contracts."

46. "Corporate law" is, essentially, composed of the Corporations Law (Law no. 6,404/76 and Law no. 10,303/2001), the Judicial Recovery Law (Law no. 11,101/2005), and the One Person Company (Law no. 12,441/2011). In addition to companies (named *sociedades anônimas*, or SAs), there are other types of partnership in Brazil's legal system, and the most important are "limited liability partnerships" (the most common legal entities in Brazil) and "cooperative partnerships" (important in the agribusiness sector). In a limited liability partnership, there is a partner's limitation of liability. Before the partner pays up his share, liability is limited to the partnership's capital. After the share is paid up, there is no longer any personal liability for the partner. Cooperative partnerships are regulated by Law no. 5,754/71 and by the Civil Code. They may not be organized with a view to obtaining a profit.

47. Only corporations can use the expression "company" (or the abbreviation "Cia.") at the beginning of their names (or use the abbreviation SA at the end), and only corporations may have their shares traded on a stock exchange (if they do the corporation will be regarded as an "open" company; if not it is a "closed" company). There are three types of share (ordinary, preference, and "of fruition"). Ordinary shares attribute the right to vote. Preference shares offer an advantage (priority for receiving dividends, priority in having capital reimbursed, or both of these, and other advantages are possible in "open" companies). "Fruition shares," unlike dividends, reimburse the shareholder according to the share's nominal value. After that, he can buy new shares ("fruition shares") that do not increase the company's capital. There are also rules about "administration" (a "board of directors," which is mandatory, a mandatory "audit board," and an "advisory board" that is optional for closed companies but mandatory for "open" companies). Executive directors are not liable for the company's obligations when the obligation is incurred on behalf of the company "as a consequence of a normal management action." Corporations law governs changes of corporate status ("transformation," that is a change in the type of entity, "incorporation," "merger," named "fusion," and "split," named "schism"). The Judicial Recovery Act is about the court-controlled procedure where the debtor files voluntary insolvency proceedings aiming to reorganize the company and allow it to recover from bankruptcy. This option is only open to enterprises and "entrepreneurs" (sole traders). The One Person Company Act introduces (2011) into the Brazilian law system a new entity (named *empresa individual de responsabilidade limitada* – individual enterprise with limited liability). The Capital Market Act/*Lei dos Mercados de Capitais* (no. 4,778/65) is completed by the "CVM Resolutions and Instructions." The CVM (*Comissão de Valores Mobiliários*) is the Brazilian SEC – Securities and Exchange Commission. There is only one stock exchange in Brazil (the São Paulo Stock Exchange), which merged the Mercantile and Futures Exchange in 2008 and is now BM&FBovespa.

48. Credit titles law is composed of the Promissory Note and Bill of Exchange Act/ *Lei das Promissórias e Cartas de Crédito* (Law no. 2,044/1908 and Edict no. 57,663/66 which adopts the Geneva Covention of March 1931), the Check Act/*Lei dos Cheques* (no. 7,357/85), the Duplicate Act/*Lei das Duplicatas* (Law no. 5,474/ 68), and the Promissory Note and Bill of Exchange/ Check Act, which is similar to the law in the USA and Europe. The "duplicate" is a unique credit title that is used in Brazil, especially in bank credit operations. The trader creates a title on the basis of his trades (where there is a term for the payment) and this title is sent to the bank, to anticipate resources. If the consumer does not accept the title (because there is no trade, eventually), the bank will demand that the trader replace the title, or pay for the loan.

II. Position of the Judiciary

49. Traditionally, in Brazil, as in other countries that have adopted the civil law system, statutory law is the main (if not the only) primary authority, giving the judge the role of *bouche de la loi* or voice of the law. However, recently, after the Federal Constitution of 1988, judicial precedents have gained more power. After the 45th Amendment, the concept of binding precedents was introduced into the Brazilian law system (named *súmula vinculante*), as the New Procedural Civil Code (Law no. 13,105/2015) introduced more possibility of superior courts overturning the judgments of judges at first instance, as "repetitive case incident resolution" (*incidente*

de resolução de demandas repetitivas, Article 976). These cases reinforce judicial precedent as a primary source of legal authority, giving the Brazilian judiciary a more influential position.

50. Another fact that contributes to these changes is the idea that principles are also norms, like rules, and can be applied by judges (first instance), and not only by the Supreme Court. It is important to remember that, in Brazil, there are, simultaneously, two models of judicial review of constitutional rules and principles: the centralized system (by the Supreme Court) and the decentralized system (by any judge or court). Therefore, it is possible to say that in Brazil decisions by the courts are formally considered a source of law and that there is a mixed system in which the precedents of courts must be followed by subsequent decisions.

III. Sources of Private Law in General and of Tort Law in Particular

51. Although in Brazilian tort law, the doctrine differentiates contractual liability from "extra-contractual" liability, when the Civil Code discusses "civil liability," this includes both contractual and extra-contractual liability. Therefore, it is impossible to fully separate "contracts" and "torts," because they belong to the same "liability system." Following the tradition of civil law systems in Brazil, an "integrative" category ("obligation") applies to both contractual and extra-contractual liability. In addition, in Brazilian law system "public liability" (the liability imposed on public agents) has specific principles and rules. There is no civil trial by jury and all civil liability cases are decided by a judge or a court ("technical judgment").

§3. FUNCTION OF THE LAW OF TORTS

52. Every tort law system must have a reason to exist and must develop a certain function, given that nothing justifies the fact of incurring the costs of transferring harm simply for the transfer's sake. In brief, a tort law system has two basic functions, reparation and prevention, to which may be added two ancillary functions, sanctions and information. It may be concluded, in summary, that tort law serves the relevant function of maximization of welfare.[60]

53. The core function of reparation is developed by tort law, characterized fundamentally by the obligation to compensate for the harm caused, by offering to victims proportionate compensation for the harm they have suffered. This is the tenor of the traditional legal perspective. As Shavell highlights,[61] "the great majority of lawyers, attorneys, judges and, probably, citizens, assume that equitable and proportionate compensation to victims for harm is the main function of accident liability." In fact, throughout history, the tort law system has been presented as an

---

60. *See* BATTESINI, *Direito e Economia, Novos Horizontes no Estudo da Responsabilidade Civil no Brasil,* 2011, São Paulo, at 103.
61. *See* SHAVELL, Foundations of Economic Analysis of Law, 2004, Cambridge, at 267.

efficient mechanism of reparation for the harm caused to victims. In addition, even today, of the many existing accident resolution systems, tort law is still is the best, if not the only, system for compensation of harm. However, contemporary society has registered the development of superior mechanisms to secure compensation and this has led to this traditional function of tort law losing its importance. The insurance system in particular has been seen as a more effective mechanism in reparation, acting with more celerity and fewer costs than the tort law system.[62] Moreover, today the reparation function is not an exclusive feature of tort law, it being developed jointly or alternatively with other mechanisms in the case of accidents. Therefore, the other functions of civil liability are being seen in a new light.[63]

54. From the social perspective, it can be inferred that, when reparation is made, the harm caused by the accident does not go away: it is only transferred from the victim to the perpetrator. It does not really return matters to a prior state, but only transfers the harm. Schäfer and Ott add that, "the compensatory principle is not enough as a guide" for a civil liability system, it being "a mistake to consider the preventive aspect of compensation for harms as a mere welcome side effect. It must be considered the most important aspect."[64] It must be considered, though, that in contemporary society, the preventive function does not constitute an exclusive feature of the tort law system. The tort law system is not the only, and is possibly, not the most powerful, instrument for preventing accidents. Insurance, *lato sensu*, and public costs are instruments with great power to reduce accidents.[65] It can be verified that today the prevention function of civil liability, by creating incentives for potential perpetrators and victims to adopt conduct that may avoid or mitigate the costs of accidents, is seen to be a consistent function of the tort law system.[66]

55. The ancillary function of punishment developed by tort law consists in the imposition on the author of monetary costs additional to the effective costs of the harm. In certain situations, to keep the incidence of accidents down to socially tolerable levels, the imposition of additional deterrent incentives such as punitive damages may be justified; the purpose is to induce preventive behavior in situations of risk, either by the perpetrator of the harmful act or by persons who find themselves in similar situations, as a general deterrent.[67] The punitive function and the compensatory function, in a tort law system, perform their primordial deterrence function according to socially desirable standards. When the compensatory function is not enough or where it is inadequate to create incentives for prevention, the punitive function is complementary. It can be inferred, therefore, that, like sanctions of

---

62. *See* PASTOR, *Derecho de Daños,* 2004, Buenos Aires, at 59.
63. *See* BATTESINI, *Direito e Economia, Novos Horizontes no Estudo da Responsabilidade Civil no Brasil,* 2011, São Paulo, at 104.
64. *See* SCHAEFFER, Hans-Bernd and OTT, Klaus. Economic Analysis of Civil Law, 2004, Cheltenham, at 110.
65. *See* PASTOR, *Derecho de Daños,* 2004, Buenos Aires, at 59.
66. *See* BATTESINI, *Direito e Economia, Novos Horizontes no Estudo da Responsabilidade Civil no Brasil,* 2011, São Paulo, at 105.
67. *See* TESTA, *Daños Punitivos, Análisis Económico del Derecho y Teoría de Juegos,* 2006, Buenos Aires, at 38–39.

a criminal nature, the punitive function developed by tort law has a deterrent effect, contributing positively to the control of accident risks.[68]

56. As a punitive function, the ancillary function of information is strongly related to the preventive function of a tort law system. As Schäfer and Ott highlight, civil liability is fundamental to the establishment of a determined standard of conduct, the standard of a rational man acting with the reasonable care required by social interaction; the norms of tort law must give guidance to potential perpetrators about what actions or behavior are or are not acceptable.[69] Tort law rules thus develop a provisional function, giving information about the least risky manner of acting and reducing asymmetries in information distribution. Using the terminology employed by Joseph Raz, tort law rules act as a "logarithmic table," as "a map that simplifies navigation."[70] Therefore, it can be inferred that, as administrative regulation norms, tort law rules give relevant information about risks and preventive measures, acting as a reference point in shaping the behavior of potential perpetrators and victims of accidents.[71]

57. By way of elucidation, Pastor has registered that tort law has experimented with extraordinary changes in the last forty years. "In its historic function, which constituted fundamentally a proportionate mechanism of compensation in favor of victims and to deter harmful activities, the first function (compensation) does not seem to be as important as before."[72] Currently, as the author agrees, the value of a tort law system must be assessed by the results given by the performance of the prevention function in situations in which other mechanisms of compensation cannot act or when they do act, are inferior in their reparatory function. Therefore, tort law performs a relevant social welfare function, characterized by "minimizing the costs of accidents, which are: the probable expected harm; the costs of adopting precautions; the costs of supporting the risk; and the administrative costs of the adopted system." In other words, the social welfare function is characterized by maximizing the benefits proportionate to the activities involving the risk of accidents, or the total benefits to society deducting the social costs of accidents.[73]

58. Considering the current scope of tort law in Brazil, with the advent of the 2002 Brazilian Civil Code, the idea can be affirmed that civil liability performs a function in promoting social welfare.[74] In this particular, by discussing the fundamental principles that led to the formulation of the Civil Code of 2002, Reale, the

---

68. *See* BATTESINI, Direito e Economia, *Novos Horizontes no Estudo da Responsabilidade Civil no Brasil,* 2011, São Paulo, at 105.
69. *See* SCHAEFFER, Hans-Bernd and OTT, Klaus, *The Economic Analysis of Civil Law,* 2004, Cheltenham, at 113.
70. *See* RAZ, Practical Reasons and Norms, 1999, Oxford, at 60.
71. *See* BATTESINI, *Direito e Economia, Novos Horizontes no Estudo da Responsabilidade Civil no Brasil,* 2011 São Paulo, at 106.
72. *See* PASTOR, *Derecho de Daños,* 2004, Buenos Aires, at 102.
73. *See* BATTESINI, *Direito e Economia, Novos Horizontes no Estudo da Responsabilidade Civil no Brasil,* 2011, São Paulo, at 107.
74. *See Ibid.,* at 107–108.

coordinator of the commission responsible for the Code, highlights ethnicity, operability and sociability as indicating the "influence of the social upon the individual," as well as highlighting "the constant goal of the new Code as a way to counteract the manifest individualist character of the Civil Code of 1916."[75]

§4. Relationship Between Tort and Criminal Law

59. The Brazilian legal system distinguishes between tort law and criminal law. Brazilian criminal law is codified in the Criminal Code of 1940 (Decree-Law no. 2,848, of December 7, 1940), which, in its general part, establishes the general rules of application of criminal law, and in the special part, lists all acts that constitute crimes in Brazil, classifying them into the following categories: crimes against the person, crimes against property, crimes against intangible property, crimes against organization of labor, crimes against religious feelings, crimes against respect for the dead, crimes against sexual dignity, crimes against the family, crimes against bodily integrity, crimes against peace, faith, and public administration. In addition to the modalities predicted in the Criminal Code, other crimes are defined in special legislation, namely: bankruptcy crimes (Bankruptcy and Law Judicial Reorganization Law – Law no. 11,101, of February 9, 2005), crimes against consumer relations (the Consumer's Defense Code (CDC) – Law no. 8,078, of September 11, 1990), election-related crimes (the Election Code – Law no. 4,737, of July 15, 1965), traffic crimes (the Brazilian Traffic Code – Law no. 9,503, of September 23, 1997), environmental crimes (Law no. 9,605, of February 12, 1998), among others. In addition to the Criminal Code of 1940 and special legislation typifying criminal conduct, the Criminal Procedure Code (Decree-Law no. 3,689, of October 3, 1941) provides the rules for criminal enforcement and lawsuits.

60. Criminal law has as its goal to repress infractions seen as especially reprehensible, and therefore against the interests of society. While it is a part of public law, criminal law is about the sanctions imposed by the state, the main institution responsible for criminal prosecution, which is performed through a public ministry. A criminal sanction is proportioned to the nature of the crime, its gravity, the agent's personal characteristics, and other aspects. Criminal sanctions are applied with the goal of criminalizing the perpetrator, as they have the goal of preventing new offenses being committed by the offender, "specific prevention," or by other persons, "general prevention."[76] Tort law, on the other hand, is a part of private law, acting on behalf of specific subjects whose interests have been violated by an illicit act performed by a third party. In essence, tort law constitutes itself as a legal instrument of harm allocation, based on the study of criteria for selected situations whether the harm caused to third parties should be compensated (and when it should

---

75. *See* REALE, *Visão Geral do Novo Código Civil*, 2004, São Paulo, at 12–17.
76. *See* NORONHA, *Direito das Obrigações*, 2010, São Paulo, at 532–533.

be compensated) and of the criteria for the performance of the compensatory obligation (how to compensate).[77] The main purpose of tort law, according to Zweigert and Kötz, consists in specifying, among the wide range of everyday events that lead to harm, where the harm should be transferred from the victim to the perpetrator, according to the ideals of justice and fairness that are dominant in society.[78] Even though it also includes the basic function of prevention and the ancillary functions of punishment and information, concisely, civil liability emphasizes the compensatory function, based on the idea of restoring the situation before the harmful fact occurred.

61. Though a legal fact may generate, at the same time, civil and criminal liabilities, these are independent of each other. Since they have a different legal nature, the concepts act in distinct realms. In the Brazilian legal system, the independence of tort law and criminal law is seen in Article 935 of the Civil Code of 2002. It is, though, a relative independence: many legal norms establish a connection between the two systems. Article 935 itself establishes that it will not be possible "to question the fact's existence, or who its perpetrator is, when these questions have been decided by the criminal courts." Furthermore, in terms of Article 63 of the Criminal Procedure Code, with the res judicata of the sentence, it is possible to obtain in the civil sphere an execution to compensate for the harm.[79]

§5. RELATIONSHIP BETWEEN CONTRACTUAL AND DELICTUAL OR TORTIOUS RESPONSIBILITY

62. The Brazilian Civil Code of 2002 provides a sharp distinction between torts and contract relations. Contractual relationships are regulated by the Brazilian Civil Code of 2002, in Title V, Book I – Law of Obligations, from the special part, in Articles 421–480, which establish dispositions about contracts in general and in Title VI of the same book, Articles 481–853, which regulate the diverse species of contracts: buying and selling, exchange, lease contracts, donation, lending, services performance, construction, deposit, mandate, commission, agency, and distribution; real estate management, transportation, insurance, finance, games and gambles, bail, transactions, and compromises. In addition to the modalities set out by the Civil Code, other contracts are regulated by special legislation, namely: agricultural contracts (Decree no. 59,566, of November 14, 1966), labor contracts (Labor Law Consolidation (CLT) – Decree-Law no. 5,452, of May 1, 1943), and franchising (Law no. 8,955, of December 15, 1994), among others.

63. The Brazilian legal system distinguishes between contractual responsibility and criminal or tortious responsibility. In contractual liability, the compensatory obligation bases itself on the contractual fault, in violation of a legal duty implicit

---

77. See BATTESINI, *Tort Law and Economic Development: Strict Liability in Legal Practice,* ALACDE, 2015, at 6, available at http://laijle.alacde.org/journal/vol1/iss1/2.
78. See ZWEIGERT & KÖTZ, *Introducción al Derecho Comparado,* 2002, México, at 660.
79. See DINIZ, *Curso de Direito Civil Brasileiro, Responsabilidade Civil,* 2009, São Paulo, at 25–26.

in the legal business entered into between the parties. There is a preexisting legal relation, the contract, which defines the duties that the parties must carry out, and the obligation to pay damages originating from the fault. In criminal or tortious responsibility, the obligation to compensate harm caused originates from a transgression of a legal duty imposed by law, based on respect for persons and the things of others, the general duty of *neminem laedere*.[80] In fact, as Cavalieri Filho highlights, the division between contractual and criminal liability is not stable; on the contrary, there is a real symbiosis between these two kinds of liability, since some rules stated by the 2002 Brazilian Civil Code for contractual liability are also applicable to tortious liability.[81]

§6. PROTECTED INTERESTS

64. A wide field of interests is protected by the Brazilian torts system, with emphasis on the protection of absolute interests, the person and property rights. The systematic organization of harms susceptible to protection under civil liability is a task traditionally carried out by legal theory, it being possible to identify some categories of harm, namely: personality rights offenses; property rights offenses; offenses in family situations, which generate maintenance rights; offenses in factual situations; and offenses to duties imposed by the general principle of good faith.[82]

65. Personality rights, in essence, have as their goal to uphold the respect for life, health, image, name, thought, honor, liberty, and other characteristics of human persons. The general principles applicable to personality rights are expressly stated in Articles 11–21 of the Civil Code of 2002. In addition, many dispositions of the Code establish the rules of tort law applicable to the violation of personality rights, referring expressively to homicide, in Article 948; injuries and offenses to health, in Articles 949 and 950; personal injuries, defamation and calumny, in Article 955; and offenses against personal liberty, in Article 954.[83]

66. Property rights are those which attribute a direct and immediate power over a thing, which is enforceable with regard to third parties. Property rights are the object of express legal prediction in Book III, Titles II to X, of the Civil Code of 2002, extensive regulation of property rights being highlighted in Articles 1228–1368. Offenses to property rights have a special place in the harms caused to the movable and real estate property of others, which are widely regulated under civil liability in Articles 186, 187, 927, 942, and 944 of the Civil Code.[84]

67. Another category of harm that causes civil liability are offenses to family situations that generate the obligations of maintenance, such as are set out in Article

---

80. *See* NORONHA, *Direito das Obrigações*, 2010, São Paulo, at 451–453 and 523–525.
81. *See* CAVALIERI FILHO, *Programa de Responsabilidade Civil*, 2010, São Paulo, at 15–16.
82. *See* NORONHA, *Direito das Obrigações*, 2010, São Paulo, at 465–466.
83. *See Ibid.*, at 466–467, and NADER, *Curso de Direito Civil, Responsabilidade Civil*, 2014, Rio de Janeiro, at 94–95.
84. *See Ibid.*, at 467.

948, II, of the Civil Code: "in case of homicide, the damages consist … in the payment of maintenance to persons to whom the deceased owed it, taking into account the probable life span of the victim." In the Brazilian legal system, family law is regulated in Book IV of the Civil Code of 2002, of which the theme is maintenance, set out in Articles 1694–1710.[85]

68. Some offenses against factual situations justify protection under civil liability. This is the case with possession, regulated by the Book III, Title I, of the Civil Code of 2002, where disturbance or dispossession by third parties authorizes the possessor to demand damages for the damage suffered, in the terms of Article 1212 of the Civil Code. Another situation that fits in this category is the preservation of maintenance that one of a couple gives to the other in parafamiliar unions of same-sex persons and cohabitation, according to Article 1727 of the Civil Code.[86]

69. The legal duty to act according to good faith in social relations is established by the Brazilian legal system in Article 422 of the Civil Code of 2002, which states: "the contractors are obliged to observe, in the conclusion of the contract, and in its execution, the principles of probity and good faith." This constitutes, as Fernando Noronha emphasizes, the positive aspect of the general principle of objective good faith, namely that "each person must act in social relations according to certain socially recommended minimum standards of conduct, of loyalty, correction and fairness, which correspond to the legitimate expectations of others."[87] Offenses against the duties imposed by the general principle of good faith are qualified as illicit, in the terms of Article 187 of Civil Code of 2002, thus justifying the application of civil liability to both contr actual or extra-contractual faults, prior to, contemporary with, or after the contract's performance.

---

85. *See* NORONHA, *Direito das Obrigações*, São Paulo, 2010, at 467, NADER, Curso de Direito Civil, Responsabilidade Civil, 2014, Rio de Janeiro, at 242–249.
86. *See Ibid.*, at 468–469, and *Ibid.*, at 269–275 and 360.
87. *See* NORONHA, *Direito das Obrigações*, 2010, São Paulo, at 470–473.

Part I. Liability for One's Own Acts

Chapter 1. General Principles

§1. UNLAWFULNESS AND FAULT

70. In tort law, behavior contrary to the law (unlawfulness) is a necessary element (or assumption). There cannot be liability unless an act or fact can be considered unlawful. In interpersonal relations it is reasonable to suppose that situations in which interests conflict may occur, often provoking interferences that may cause harm to one or both subjects' rights in this relation. However, not all relations of this kind cause liability; many conform to the legal patterns established by society. For instance, during a procurement bid for a contract with public authorities, a bidder takes advantage of the other by putting forward a better proposal, which logically causes harm to the defeated party; however, if the procedure is formally regulated it will not generate any compensation obligation to that party. The same rationale applies when a driver gets the last spot in a parking lot, preventing access to other drivers; in the same way, harm is caused to those who cannot park, although since this behavior is not unlawful, no one incurs any liability as a result.

71. As Mello notes:[88]

> an act contrary to the law is not sufficient, by itself, to characterize it as illicit. In truth, there are situations, that, despite being, by their nature, contrary to law, since they cause a minor harm, are not illicit. Namely, to kill or cause bodily injury in self-defense necessarily provokes harm to the other (Civil Code of 2002, Article 188, I and II; Criminal Code, Article. 23), as a damage-led fact act. In these cases, the contrariety to law is not illicit; thus such acts have effects other than those proper to illicit activities.

72. The notion of the illicit can be extracted from the rules in Articles 186 and 187 of the CCB. In Article 186 can be found the definition of subjective ILLICIT-NESS, which originates from the agent's conduct (fault) which causes harm, even though this damage has no economic content. As for Article 187, it states other grounds for illicitness, such as the abuse of rights. In this case, the illicitness has a strict liability nature, and the agent's conduct is thus independent of fault verification. However, there may be civil liability with no illicit activity; thus there is in

---

88. *See* MELLO, *Teoria do Fato Jurídico – Plano da Existência*, 2003, São Paulo, at 219.

law an express preclusion of the illicit (which does not remove the contrariety to the law, or unlawfulness). As there may be illicit activities with no civil liability, thus the act or fact is not imputable to determine agency (§5, and following paragraphs).

§2. CONCEPT OF FAULT

73. A fault comprises voluntary conduct contrary to the duty of care imposed by the law, producing either an unintended harmful event, either foreseen or foreseeable (in a narrow sense/*stricto sensu*/, fault or negligent harm) or an intended one (intentional harm). According to Diniz:[89]

> fault in a broad sense is a violation of a legal duty, imputable to a person, according to an intentional fact or omission of due diligence or care, which comprises: the intention, or intentional damage to a legal duty, the narrow sense liability, fault "stricto sensu", characterized by malpractice, imprudence or negligence, without any thought of violating a duty … The intention is the conscious will to violate the law, directed to an illicit end, and the fault includes MALPRACTICE, imprudence and negligence.

74. As Rodrigues reminds us:[90]

> the problem with defining fault, which is the object of debate in foreign literature, where the exact meaning of the word "faute" is under discussion (the expression can be found in Article 1.382 of the Napoleonic Code), is less ambiguous among us. That is because, regarding the aquillian liability of Article 186 of the Brazilian Civil Code, it defines what is comprehended by the negligent behavior of the agent performing the harmful act.

75. The notion of what is a "voluntary action or omission, negligence or imprudence" which is quoted in Article 186 was coined in a masterly fashion by Dias,[91] from Article 159 of the Civil Code of 1916 which had identical content:

> From fault, characterized … as negligence or imprudence can be derived other notions that demand a closer look. Thus in this title are, in effect, comprehended negligence, imprudence and malpractice, which are all related to a nuclear element: the lack of diligence, prevention or care. Negligence is the omission of what is usually done, adjusted to the emergent conditions that rule the regular conduct of human business. It is the lack of observance of norms that require us to operate with caution, capacity, solicitude and mindfulness. It

---

89. *See* DINIZ, *Curso de Direito Civil Brasileiro*, 2009, São Paulo, at 41.
90. *See* RODRIGUES, *Direito Civil, vol. 4 – Responsabilidade Civil*, 2002, São Paulo, at 146/147.
91. *See* DIAS, *Da Responsabilidade Civil*, 2006, Rio de Janeiro, at 135.

consists of imprudence in precipitate, thoughtless and careless action in contradiction to the norms of rational procedure. It is recklessness in acting, omission of the caution with which we should act. Omission and abstinence are used abusively as synonyms, despite their perceivable difference. Omission is negligence, the act of forgetting the rules of procedure, in carrying out activity, while abstinence is inactivity. Generically speaking, omission assumes an initiative; abstinence excludes it.

The same occurs with omission and inertia. Both concepts have a negative procedural meaning, although omission has a broader and more complex meaning. In essence, it is fault. However, there are distinctive differences between them.

Negligence is related mainly to dissent; imprudence is connected, more than to any other concept, to recklessness, like malpractice, originally to a lack of a required skill.

76. It is always advisable to remember that, in the form determined by Article 935 of the Civil Code, tort law is independent of criminal law, from which results the fact that the standard for determining fault is different in the two legal branches. The criteria to define fault in criminal law will always be more precise than those required in private law. Therefore, the non-characterization of a conduct as faulty in criminal law will not affect the possibility of the same conduct being considered to incur civil liability.

§3. DUTY OF CARE

77. The duty of care may be related to the agent's omission regarding activity that, if adopted, might have prevented the harmful event (negligence), or to the active behavior of the agent acting hastily, without sufficient consideration of the consequences of his/her conduct (recklessness imprudence), or further, when the damage is due to non-observance of technical standards (malpractice or ignorance).

§4. CAPACITY

78. The notion "illicit" would not be complete without a legal system recognizing, in addition to unlawfulness, the possibility of an act or fact being tied to a particular agent; this is called "imputability." Direito and Cavalieri Filho,[92] commenting on Article 928 of the Civil Code, clarify that:

As highlighted, there is no liability without the neglect of a legal duty, which is expressed through an illicit act. That implies, firstly, the existence of this duty, and, therefore, the issuing of a command to free beings, who acknowledge it and obey it; secondly, in the voluntary practice of a conduct different

---

92. *See* DIREITO & CAVALIERI FILHO, *Comentários ao Novo Código Civil*, 2007, Rio de Janeiro, at 185.

from what is demanded by law. There is no such violation, as Fernando Pessoa Jorge well observes, when an agent acts without intelligence or will. In order for an illicit act to be a violation of a duty, it is necessary that the agent is in command of his/her mental faculties, in such a manner that his/her acts can be morally attributed or imputable to that agent. The violation of duty implies in the agent the quality of imputability (Ensaio sobre os Pressupostos da Responsabilidade Civil, Lisboa, 1968, p. 68).

To impute is to attribute to someone the liability for something. Imputability is, thus, the bundle of personal conditions that gives the agent the capacity to be responsible for the consequences of conduct contrary to a duty; an imputable person is someone who could and should have acted differently.

From that it can be concluded that imputability is an assumption, not only of fault in a broad sense, but of liability itself. Therefore, it can be stated that there is no way for a person to be liable for the practice of a harmful act if, at the moment it was carried out, he/she did not have the capacity to comprehend the reprehensible character of his/her conduct and make a decision according to this rationale.

There are two elements of imputability: maturity and mental sanity. The first concerns mental development and the second, its health.

Consequently, an agent is imputable if he is mentally sane and developed, and capable of comprehending the character of his/her conduct and acts with this comprehension.

79. During the whole period when the Civil Code of 1916 was in force, the opinion prevailed that incapable persons, being non-imputable, could not be civilly liable. The changes introduced by the Civil Code of 2002, in the highlighted Article 928, have permitted the liability of an incapable person (mentally disabled and/or under the age of 18 years), through mitigation and subsidiarity criteria. An incapable person will not be responsible for harms caused by him/her to people if the person responsible for him/her has no obligation to repair the damages of if the incapable person does not have sufficient wealth to provide compensation. The generic non-imputability, here, is void by virtue of an exceptional norm that sets out the notion of the victim compensation, which contradicts the protective rule of the incapable.

80. According to Diniz,[93] "the imputability element that constitutes the fault is due to the personal conditions (conscience and intent) of the person who practiced the harmful act, in a fashion that consists of the possibility of doing something as an act proceeding from free will." The author recognizes as "exceptions to imputability" the situations of underage and demented persons (incapable); in the case of Article 928, thus, even with imputability there is civil liability.

---

93. *See* DINIZ, *Curso de Direito Civil Brasileiro*, 2009, São Paulo, at 45.

Chapter 2. Specific Cases of Liability

§1. LIABILITY OF PROFESSIONALS

81. In the case of professional activities, the distinction between liabilities arising from the breach of contractual obligations (which are not the subject of this study) and those resulting from the violation of absolute duties must first be established (or civil liability *stricto sensu*). Any service performed by a professional will create contractual obligations, despite the fact that a contract is mutually beneficial. However, we will examine only civil liability, which has its origins in an act (licit or illicit) that is not framed as negotiable by its nature (breaches of obligation would thus be translated into the relatively illicit). Aligning with criminal liability, in administrative liability (agency and syndicate controls of professional performance), and distinguished from contractual liability, is the civil liability (*stricto sensu*) of professionals in a specific situation. Such regulation has its origin essentially in the rules and principles found in the Brazilian Civil Code, along with situations in the domain of the Consumer Protection Code (Law no. 8,078/90).

I. In General: Standard of Care for "Experts"

82. The Brazilian Civil Code (Article 186), unlike the Criminal Code (Article 18, II), does not include malpractice as a form of fault. However, as Theodoro Junior emphasizes,[94] "that does not mean that malpractice is not a form of fault leading to civil liability," malpractice not being distinct from negligence and recklessness. What really defines malpractice in particular, is the existence, regarding the imputable agent, of technical, specific, knowledge, which is not required in other cases of negligence and recklessness.

83. The notion is more common among the doctrine that "malpractice is found when the harm has its origin in the nonobservance of technical norms,"[95] or, as Coelho states,[96] "it is a non-intentional fault in professional or job performance;" its relevance arises from professional liability. A recent example of technical associated professional liability is predicted in the General Data Protection Law (LGPD)[97] in which liability is due to a "controller" or "operator" who is liable for causing harm to another by a failure in the personal data treatment of the victim.

84. The standards for defining malpractice can vary from case to case, and depend fundamentally on technical criteria, which are found in the rules generally issued by agencies supervising the exercise of the professions (for instance, the

---

94. *See* THEODORO JUNIOR, *Comentários ao Novo Código Civil*, 2003, Rio de Janeiro, at 106.
95. *See* NADER, *"Curso de Direito Civil, vol. 7 – Responsabilidade Civil,"* 2014, Rio de Janeiro, at 92.
96. *See* COELHO, *Curso de Direito Civil, vol. 2*, 2005, São Paulo, at 309.
97. *See* BRASIL, *Congresso Nacional. Lei 13.709 de 14 de Agosto de 2018, art.* 42.

Medicine National Council,[98] the Brazilian BAR Association – OAB,[99] the Federal Council of Engineering, Agronomy and Urbanism,[100] and the Architecture Council of Brazil[101]).

II. Medical Practitioners

85. Medical practitioners' liability is considered, according to Borges, as part of the general system of liability, though it is legally tied to the consumer law system; as Borges states,[102] medical civil liability obeys the same principles as general tort law, according to which someone who performs a particular act or carries out an intention, or even by "simple fault," causes harm, has to repair it. Liability requires a fault, or a finding that the practitioner was not in compliance with essential legal duties originating from the performance of medical services, which is itself a fault, in any of its varieties (negligence, malpractice, or recklessness), or did not intend to fulfill such obligations. As the author further states,[103] the inference can be drawn that "extra-contractual liability is configured by the facts connecting the doctor and the patient, the former having the duty to provide medical assistance, for instance in an emergency … ."

86. The main consequence of this distinction lies in the distribution of the burden of proof; thus contractual medical liability is tied to consumer law, in which, despite the rule contained in §4 of Article 14 of Law no. 8,078/90, the inversion of the burden of proof is common, based upon VIII of Article 6 of the same law. This distinction, however, was mitigated with the emergence of the new Brazilian Procedure Code. In its Article 373, §1, the Code sets out the possibility (in cases laid down in law or in the face of peculiarities of causation related to the difficulty or impossibility of achieving the goal … or better conditions for achieving proof of the contrary fact) for the judge to redistribute the burden of proof, "if this makes for a fundamental decision." Diniz[104] gives as examples fake medical certificates that authorize – it could deter what constitutes a liability for omission – a person who is not qualified to practice medicine, or not ordering the immediate removal of a wounded person in emergency situations, and others.

---

98. *See* CONSELHO FEDERAL DE MEDICINA. *Código de Ética Médica.* Available at http://portal.cfm.org.br.
99. *See* ORDEM DOS ADVOGADOS DO BRASIL, *Estatuto da OAB.* Available at http://www.oab.org.br.
100. *See* CONSELHO FEDERAL DOS ENGENHEIROS E AGRONOMIA. *Código de Ética Profissional.* Available at http://www.confea.org.br.
101. *See* CONSELHO DOS ARQUITETOS E URBANISTAS DO BRASIL. *Código de Ética e Disciplina dos Arquitetos e Urbanistas.* Available at http://www.caubr.gov.br.
102. *See* BORGES, *Erro Médico nas Cirurgias Plásticas*, 2014, São Paulo, at 211.
103. *Ibid.* Where it is said that "the personal liability of the liberal professionals will be verified only through analysis of fault," at 214.
104. *See* DINIZ, *Curso de Direito Civil Brasileiro, vol. 7 – Responsabilidade Civil,* 2009, São Paulo, at 296.

III. Legal Practitioners

87. In the case of attorneys, civil liability is also mainly of a contractual nature; but there are situations where a professional can be charged with violation of an absolute duty, even if a contractual bond is lacking. This would include, for instance, offenses in the exercise of a profession towards another professional, a judge or justice official, where the relationship of representation of a client is absent.

IV. Builders and Architects

88. In Brazil, civil liability is generically governed by Article 927 of the Brazilian Civil Code; however so-called "consumer relations" are set out in the CDC. "Consumer" relations are considered to be those entered into between consumers and suppliers, according to the CDC: "Art. 2° The consumer is every physical or legal person who acquires or use products or services at their final destination," as well as the plurality of persons who may enter into these relations, as the text of the same article refers to "the collective of persons, even though indeterminable, who take part in consumer relations." Suppliers are defined in Article 3: "A supplier is any physical or legal person, public or private, national or foreigner, such as the entities that carry out production, assembly, creation, construction, transformation, importing, exporting, distributing or commercializing products or services." As may be observed, the activities of creation and construction, having a physical or legal person as their final destination, make up, according to Brazilian law, consumer relations.

89. Therefore, builders' and architects' liability falls under the jurisdiction of the CDC, and not the general statements of the Brazilian Civil Code of 2002, by the criteria of the specificity of the applicable law, according to current jurisprudence.[105] The substantial distinction between builders' and architects' liability can be found in different kinds of factual relations, where there is a builder company and a liberal professional architect. If the architect is hired to do the plans by the builder he is held liable for the execution of the project; or both builders and architect may be hired separately by the consumer.

90. According to current jurisprudence, the architect's liability is set out in Article 14 §4 of the CDC, and is considered an instance of a "liberal professional's liability," where "the personal liability of liberal professionals will be configured through the verification of fault," while the builder's liability is set out by the article's caput: "The supplier of services responds, independently of fault, by compensation for the harm caused to the consumer by defects in the performance of services, as also for giving insufficient information about their nature and risks." Therefore, the first distinction that can be made about architects' and builders' liability, throughout the reading of Article 14 of the CDC, is that the former is liable

---

105. *See* TJRS. AC, N° 70016450728. *Nona Câmara Cível. Comarca de Porto Alegre.* Des.ª Iris Helena Medeiros Nogueira. 08/12/2006. Porto Alegre.

through the institute of negligence, and the latter is liable through strict liability, through the risks created, the proof of fault not being necessary, only the cause and the harm itself, for the obligation to pay compensatory damages to arise.

91. In addition, in the case of hiring of a liberal professional for the building company, the architect's liability is joined with that of the builder regarding the plan and its execution defects;[106] if the architect hires the building team, he/she will be liable for all the details originating from his supervisory duties and conformities with the plan. And, finally, in the case of separately contracted architects and builders, the architect's liability will be restricted to defects in the plans as the builders will answer for defects connected with non-conformities with the plan.[107]

92. As for the burden of proof, Cavalieri Filho states that, "As highlighted above, liberal professionals, as they are performers of services, are not outside the discipline of the CDC. The only exception that is made for them concerns strict liability. And it was necessary to make this exception; thus they are subject to the other principles of the CDC – information, transparency, good faith and the reversal of the burden of proof, etc."[108] In this way, it is the responsibility of the liberal professional to prove that there are no non-conformities with the plan that generated the harm or that the plan itself was not defective according to the technology available; the builder must do the same in turn, given the statement in Article 6, VIII.

§2. LIABILITY OF PUBLIC AUTHORITIES (GOVERNMENTAL LIABILITY)

93. Under Brazilian law, public authorities and private persons providing public services are civilly liable for harm caused by a third party acting as their official representative, even while they have sovereign public immunity. This widely accepted principle is currently undisputed and it is the object of a constitutional provision. In the terms of Article 37, §6, of the Federal Constitution, "the legal persons of public law, and private law performing public services, will be liable for the harm caused by their agents, third parties having a right of redress against those responsible in cases of intention or fault." An analogous disposition can be found in Article 43 of the Civil Code of 2002: "the legal persons of internal public law are civilly liable for the acts of their agents that cause harm to third parties, who have a right of redress against those who caused the harm, if fault or intention can be attributed to them." An important change occurred with the entry into force of Law no. 13,655, of April 25, 2018, since, in the wording given to Article 28 of Decree-Law no. 4,657, of September 4, 1942 (entitled "Introduction Law to the Norms of Brazilian Law"), "the public agent will be personally responsible for its decisions or technical opinions in case of intent or gross error." With this wording, any possibility of

---

106. *See* TJRS. AC, N° 70018927665. *Nona Câmara Cível. Comarca de Rio Grande.* Des.ª Marilene Bonzanini Bernardi. 26/12/2007. Porto Alegre.
107. *See* TJRS. RI, N° 71001305770. *Primeira Turma Recursal Cível. Comarca de Guaíba.* Dr. Ricardo Torres Hermann. 04/10/2007. Porto Alegre.
108. *See* CAVALIERI FILHO, *Programa de Responsabilidade Civil.* 2010, São Paulo.

personal responsibility of public agents for simple fault, or, more than that, of their responsibility without fault, is ruled out.[109]

94. As can be inferred from Article 37, §6, of the Federal Constitution, for public authorities to be responsible civilly for an act performed in the realm of public administration, a few requisites must be fulfilled. The occurrence of a harm is necessary, it not being sufficient for the payment of compensation that the administrative act was illicit. The harmful conduct must be attributed to an officer or agent of the legal person of public law or private law performing the public service. The agent, in carrying out the act, must do it while exercising his public function and not in his/her private life. There must be a nexus of causation between the harmful conduct and the verified harm. Moreover, the administrative act must be illicit.[110]

95. Regarding the illicit nature of the act and the imputation nexus, the prevalent theory in Brazilian law distinguishes between acts of commission and acts of omission. Regarding the former, there is a consensus that the state's liability is objective (strict liability), founded on the theory of administrative risk by Article 37, §6 of the Federal Constitution. As for acts of omission, doctrine[111] and jurisprudence diverge between the adoption of strict liability[112] and the negligence system, founded in the theory of *faute du service.*[113]

96. The following are applicable to the state's liability: the exemption clauses of self-defense, the regular exercise of a right, and damage or destruction of another's belongings or harm to a person in order to protect them greater imminent harm (Article 188 of the Civil Code of 2002); causation exemption clauses, such as chance, act of God and exclusive victim's fault (doctrinal and jurisprudential construction); and the reduction of the value of the damage by the contributory fault of the victim (Article 945 of the Civil Code). In addition, when the admitted negligence is fundamental, the liability of the state is not admitted in cases where the public office or agent acts without intention or fault *stricto sensu.*[114]

---

109. *See* BINENBOJM, Gustavo; CYRINO, Andrew. "Article 28 of LINDB – The general clause of administrative mistake," Administrative Law Magazine, Rio de Janeiro, Special Edition: Public Law in the Law of Introduction to the Rules of Brazilian Law – LINDB (Law n. 13.655/2018), pp. 203–224, November 2018.

110. *See* NADER, *Curso de Direito Civil, Responsabilidade Civil,* 2014, Rio de Janeiro, at 319–320, and RODRIGUES JUNIOR, MAMEDE and ROCHA, *Responsabilidade Civil Contemporânea,* 2011, São Paulo, at 403–409.

111. *See* CAVALIERI FILHO, *Programa de Responsabilidade Civil, 2010,* São Paulo, at 246–247 and 251–255, and SEVERO, *Tratado da Responsabilidade Pública,* 2009, São Paulo, at 166–168.

112. *See* STF, 2ª Turma, RE 180.602-8/SP, Relator Ministro Marco Aurélio, DJ 16.04.1999, at 1018. Brasília.

113. *See* STF, 1ª Turma, RE 170.014-9/SP, Relator Ministro Ilmar Galvão, DJ 13.02.1998, at 633. Brasília.

114. *See* NADER, *Curso de Direito Civil, Responsabilidade Civil,* 2014, Rio de Janeiro, at 331–332, and RODRIGUES JUNIOR, MAMEDE and ROCHA, *Responsabilidade Civil Contemporânea,* 2011, São Paulo, at 410–412.

97. The spectrum of application of the state's civil liability is wide, covering administrative acts practiced in the three power spheres, the legislative, the judiciary and mainly, the executive; legal demands founded on omissions by the state in the performance of public services in fields such as health, public security, infrastructure and transportation are thus frequent.[115]

§3. ABUSE OF RIGHTS (CIVIL RIGHTS)

98. Along with the subjective illicit acts described in Article 186, the Civil Code defines a situation of strict liability when the holder of a right exercises it in an abusive manner, exceeding the limits imposed by the economic or social purpose of the activity, by good faith or by social custom (Article 187). As Nader says:[116]

> according to Article 187 of the Civil Code, innovative in legislative terms and having its source in Article 334 of the Portuguese Civil Code, it is illicit to exercise a right in a manner that does not respect the limits given by its economic or social purposes, by good faith or by social custom. With the breach of any of these rules the legal figure of abuse of rights emerges, which subjects the agent to civil liability. The illicit act occurs when the agent, in exercising his right, intends to cause harm to another, this being the major aim of his conduct.

Furthermore,[117] it emerges from the content of the 37th statement of the *First Private Law Journal* (*I Jornada de Direito Civil*), promoted by the Federal Justice Council (*Conselho da Justiça Federal*): "therefore, it can be interpreted that the abuse of rights is prior to the element of fault: the civil liability based on abuse of rights is independent of fault and is based only on the end-goal criteria."

99. In his monograph on the subject Miragem[118] clarifies the difficulties of the reconstruction and conception of a new theory of abuse of rights in Brazil through Article 187 of the Civil Code:

> An apparent difficulty in considering these questions leads many scholars, including those who have dedicated themselves to the subject recently, to avoid implicitly and explicitly the connection to Article 187 of the Civil Code on the theory of the abuse of rights. In this sense, for instance, the prominent Professor Judith Martins-Costa states that, "in identifying the mentioned article of the Code as the basis for the prohibition of contradictory behavior (venire contra

---

115. *See* SEVERO, *Tratado da Responsabilidade Pública*, 2009, São Paulo, at 288 et seq. and STOCO, *Tratado de Responsabilidade Civil*, 2014, São Paulo, at 1364 et seq.
116. *See* NADER, *Curso de Direito Civil – Responsabilidade Civil*, 2014, Rio de Janeiro, at 120.
117. *Ibid.*, at 124.
118. *See* MIRAGEM, *Abuso do Direito – Proteção da Confiança e Limite ao Exercício das Prerrogativas Jurídicas no Direito Privado*, 2009, Rio de Janeiro, at 122 and following.

factum proprium), it is examined under the characterization of the inadmissible exercise of legal positions in legal reasoning identified initially by Menezes Cordeiro, regarding Portuguese Law." She justifies her rationale by considering that "the main distinction between the abuse of rights and the inadmissible exercise of a legal position, lies, therefore, in the fact that the latter does not imply fault as an element of factual support to the rule." This can be inferred from the author's preoccupation in detaching from the relation to Article 187's rules the necessity for voluntary or faulty behavior, thus deriving her rejection of this as a necessary element in an abuse of rights.

It can be inferred, though, that the conception of the abuse, exclusively through its subjective element, is nothing other than the recognition of an absolute identity between the abusive act and the emulation, which restricts its reach to the same limits as liability for fault, which goes against the tendencies of contemporary law and even the considerations that are defended and qualified by the doctrine of today.

The jurisprudence, at first, opted for a subjective conception of abuse ... Furthermore, it can be inferred that the conception of the abuse of right from its subjective angle cannot find more relevance in the doctrine, except for some recent exceptions.

The main question, though, seems to lie in the possibility of conceiving a hypothesis of strict liability, without the necessity for fault, as is the case with Article 187 of the Civil Code, and – respecting the distinctions examined above – a wide use of the concept of abuse and abusive behavior in other laws can be perceived, as occurs in the notorious case of the CDC.

100. As seen, the abuse of rights is a controversial concept because of its effect on the doctrine of strict liability and the extent of the illicit act. Miragem[119] continues his lecture on the legal nature of the abuse of rights, and its repercussions on this extension of the concept of the illicit as opposed to the institute of fault:

In current private law, thus, the illicit and the fault are not the same. The notion of civil torts, which was inherited from classic private law, gives scope for a double possibility of the illicit, which abandons the ancient concentration on the notion of fault and starts to concentrate on the violation of a legal duty. Thus, the perfect frame of strict liability, without fault, is a second general clause of the illicit in the Civil Code of 2002. This substantial alteration is part of a movement of functionalization of Brazilian private law, where the objectives and goals of legal concepts as set out in legislation are now preferred in relation to will and fault; this can be perceived easily on the grounds of the social function of many concepts such as property, contracts and firms.

This is also the rationale coined in the *Private Law Journal* (*Jornadas de Direito Civil*), promoted by the Superior Court of Justice (Superior Tribunal de Justiça – STJ) under the coordination of Minister Ruy Rosado Aguiar Júnior, who has brought together private lawyers from the whole country to examine the Civil Code, and has approved among its statements on the interpretation

---

119. *See Ibid.*

and application of the law, the 37th statement with the following content: "Art. 187. Civil liability from the abuse of rights does not depend on fault and has its basis only in objective-finalistic criteria." This means that abuse is recognized as the foundation of strict liability, and, as a corollary the possibility of an objective illicit act, with no fault, is established in the second general clause on the illicit in the new Civil Code.

Contradicting what may be supposed, given the necessity of a current comprehension of the abuse of rights that rejects intention and fault as assumptions for its characterization, it is not enough for the framing of the abuse of rights as an adequate solution to a series of situations in which the exercise of legal powers and subjective rights goes against socially acceptable behavior. In a broad sense, an apparent case of abuse of rights, such as an independent category or an illicit act in the general theory of private law, should have attributed to it two factors: (a) its wrongful recognition as a subjective liability, that requires intention or fault; (b) the great development of strict good faith as source of legal duties.

Regarding the first factor examined in detail: with regard to strict good faith and its various implications for contemporary Brazilian private law, what is needed is a comparative exercise on the abuse of rights, in order to identify its utility or not.

The development of strict good faith as a source of ancillary legal duties in Brazilian law is attributed in a great measure to the studies of Clóvis do Couto e Silva and his well-known work The Obligation as a Process. In this work, markedly inspired by German law, the Gaucho master has defined good faith, regarding the law of obligation as, "the objective maximum that determines the increasing of duties beyond those that the convention explicitly constitutes." At the same time, good faith in the strict sense identities the presence, in the law of obligation, and as well as the main duties of performance, of secondary duties and ancillary duties, oriented directly to the fulfillment of the performance (secondary) or to fulfill the contractual end and the protection of the wealth of the parties (ancillary).

101. The application of the abuse of rights is characterized as a corollary of the good faith principle, combined with the figures of exemption clauses that will be further addressed in this work:[120]

As for its application, with great utility for the evolution of the Brazilian Law, good faith has occupied a role, in terms of legal principle, mainly in the field of the law of obligations. This situation ... has led good faith to develop with great vitality among Brazilian doctrine and jurisprudence in the last two decades.

In this context, the renaissance of the abuse of rights, through the Article 187 of the Civil Code, can be questioned for its contemporaneity and utility, due mainly to the great role of good faith in the legal system prior to the Civil Code, as can be observed in Articles 113, 77, 128 and 422.

---

120. *See Ibid.*

As mentioned above, among well-known critiques of the abuse of rights, Menezes Cordeiro has said that it cannot be seen as a factor of rupture with the legal continuity brought about by the Napoleonic codification and further doctrine. In this sense, he puts forward a particular argument to demonstrate what he comprehends as the decay of the abuse of rights, rather indicating and interpreting Article 334 of the Portuguese Civil Code, based on the good faith perspective as the inadmissible exercise of a legal position. Currently, the Portuguese master is revisiting in part these positions, identifying the merits in the abuse of rights theory, particularly as an instrument of stability and correction of the legal system.

In German law, good faith fulfills this kind of corrective function of the bad exercise of liberty, perhaps in the same way as §226 of the German Civil Code (BGB), in which the abuse of rights concept is identified and established in order to condemn an emulative act (" the exercise of a right is inadmissible if it has for its end to cause harm to another"), in the same way as §826 of the BGB ("One who, in a way that goes against good customs, to inflict intentional harm on other is obliged to pay damages for the harm caused"). According to Menezes Cordeiro, §826 had two problems … the more problematic element would be that "the obligation to pay damages would deter the most adequate remedy for the inadmissible act; the cessation of the abuse itself."

It seems, though, that the simple denial of the abuse of rights in the interpretation of Article 187 of the Brazilian Civil Code (or Article 334 of the Portuguese Civil Code), does not add elements to refine the mentioned goal of the statement, which is precisely the exercise of a subjective right in an anti-social fashion. Consolidated as it is … it can be noted that, with good faith, two new concepts are incorporated, to which the doctrine and jurisprudence have paid little or no attention, either before or after the new legislation.

As mentioned above, while regarding good faith a species of effervescence in our doctrine and jurisprudence can be observed, the same cannot be said of the other two limits expressed by the rule, economic or social goals and custom. This has a greater relevance when it can be perceived that, while the matters to which it can be applied are numerous, strict good faith has an application profile fairly focused on the obligational relation, either between private parties or between private parties and the state.

102. Furthermore, Miragem addresses the social or economic function and good custom concepts in relation to the application of the abuse of rights, where:[121]

Concerning a subjective right's economic or social goal, it is true that the great debate about the theme is framed by property rights, as for the social function of ownership, mainly after the Constitution of 1988, therefore, are barely developed the social function of contracts and firms in the New Civil Code. However, it can be forgotten that as it is established by Article 187, not a few

---

121. *See Ibid.* Forense.

but all subjective rights are, according to the legislation, aiming at some economic or social goal, and therefore they must be examined from this perspective … .

The same can be said about good custom, which is a historic connection between our jurisprudence and sexual morality or a standard lifestyle, and has prejudiced the great possibilities of the concept to limit the … exercise of subjective liberty and anti-social behavior contrary to the social interest.

Therefore, the importance of Article 187 seems clear: it embodies a renewed conception of the abuse of rights, tied to the fulfillment of legal goals external to the Code, as the influence and application of constitutional rules to the legal relations of private law. This means that in the evaluation of non-conformity between the exercise of a legal situation and the values enshrined in the legal-constitutional system. In this case, the important virtue of the rediscovery of the abuse of rights is its utility as a safeguard against the consequences of the strict application of the law. As it was conceived, the concept of the abuse of rights can establish a limit to be incorporated in private law rules, on the grounds of civil liability and on other grounds of personal protection … to the constitutional rules regarding private relations, such as, for example, constitutional rules regarding personality rights, contract law, property rights and family law.

§4. INJURY TO REPUTATION AND PRIVACY

103. There is no specific legislation in Brazil which guarantees civil liability in the case of violation of human rights that may cause harm. Therefore, the normative generic fundamentals derive from the Civil Code.

104. There is a constitutional guarantee (Article 5, X) for cases of damage to or violation of intimacy, private life, honor, and personal images, all cases of the manifestation of personality rights. This constitutional warranty is evidenced by the presence of the specific chapter in Title I (of Natural Persons), of Book I (of Persons), of the general part of the Civil Code, entitled "Of Personality Rights." In this chapter, more precisely in Article 12, the rule establishes the possibility of the use of inhibitory remedies (menace or injury cessation) for the protection of personality rights, which does not imply "barriers to other sanctions set out in law." On the civil bench the liability for damages for harms caused is contemplated, including extra-patrimonial ones, on the same terms as the generic prediction defined by Article 927 of the Code. The STJ examining a situation in which it was considered possible off-balance-sheet damage due to an offense to a person's reputation, in contrast to the right to freedom of expression, understood that "the regular exercise of a right does not tolerate excesses and, therefore, the abuse of rights is a legal act, in principle a lawful object, the exercise of which, carried out without due regularity, entails a result that is considered unlawful," setting indemnity on account of the content of the did statements.[122]

§5. Interference with Contractual Relations

105. As mentioned above, in Brazilian law, in general, the line between contractual liability and extra-contractual liability is not clear; this is even more obvious in the case of professional liability. A concept's irrelevance, from the practical point of view, is also the result of similarities which can be seen in other legal systems based on the "continental model" (civil law). In Brazil, the unity of the concept of obligations is recognized (it having either contractual or extra-contractual origins), allowing this debate to be restricted to the theoretical plane.[123] Some relevance may emerge from certain effects, such as the initial term for delaying interest (if the liability is contractual, interest is counted from the warrant of the defendant; if extra-contractual, it is counted from the performance of the illicit act, according to Articles 397 and 398 of the Civil Code). There is a decision from the STJ[124] which recognizes as contractual the civil liability arising from preliminary negotiation breaches, but the matter is controversial,[125] as the decision itself acknowledges.

106. Therefore, there are cases, in professional liability, involving the recognition of a precontractual liability (and, without contract, extra-contractual), due to the violation of duties deriving from good faith (indication and clarification, help and cooperation). This possibility is more evident when a consumer relationship is in question; thus, in the terms of Law n. 8,078/90 (CDC), publicity (put out by services and product suppliers) has the nature of an offer (Article 30), being a source of liability, despite the drawing up of a contract.[126] However, there may also be an application of the strict good faith principle in situations not configured on analogical grounds, seeing that the same principle can be based on the 2002 Brazilian Civil Code.[127] With the entry into force of Law n. 13.874, of September 20, 2019

---

122. *See* STJ, REsp 1897338/DF, Rapporteur Minister Luis Felipe Salomão.
123. In the special appeal (STJ, Recurso Especial 1367955/SP), judged in 18/03/14, the Relator, Ministro PAULO SANSEVERINO, highlighted that there were no ontological differences between contractual and extra-contractual liabilities.
124. In the same Special Appeal (REsp 1367955/SP), it is stated that by legislative option, civil liability originating from negotiation breaches has a contractual nature.
125. On the topic, "preliminary negotiations and their effects," *See* LÔBO, *Direito Civil – Contratos*, 2011, São Paulo: "the discussion about whether the liability is contractual or extra-contractual or mixed was given until today. In contractual relation there is a bias towards extra-contractual liability according to the general rules of harms. In consumer relations, there is a bias in the specialized doctrine towards extra-contractual liability of a strict nature," at 86.
126. *See* STJ, *Recursos Especiais* 1199117/SP, de 18/12/12; 1261513/SP, de 27/08/13; 1344967/SP, de 26/08/14 e 1428801/RJ, de 27/10/15. Brasília.
127. In the already mentioned Special Appeal (*Recurso Especial* 1367955/SP), the Relator highlighted that the principle of strict good faith is given since obligations arise even before the carrying out of the legal business intended by the parties. In fact, before the conclusion of the legal business, factual relationships are established between the persons, called "social contacts," from which derive legal duties, whose violation implies civil liability.

(designated as the "Economic Freedom Law"), Article 50 of the Brazilian Civil Code was reworded, delimiting the cases of disregard of the legal entity, for the purpose of attributing responsibility to its partners and administrators.

Part II. Liability for Acts of Others

107. The main rule in tort is that a person is responsible for his own acts. This is what is traditionally called direct liability, simple liability, or simply liability for one's own acts, as seen in Part I of this study. In some circumstances, however, a person may be indirectly liable either for harms caused by others, also known as third-party liability, vicarious liability or simply liability for the acts of others *stricto sensu*; or for harm caused by inanimate things which are also known as the fact of things, or even by the keeping of inanimate things or simply liability for things; or for harm caused by animals, which is conventionally called animal fact liability, keeping of animals liability, or simply liability for animals.[128] As indirect liability or complex liability represents an exception to the general principle, creating a liability for a person who that did not directly cause the harm, a legally qualified element is necessary which is related to a duty of oversight, vigilance, or custody between this person and the person directly liable for the harm, or over the thing or animal which caused the direct harm.[129]

---

128. *See* NORONHA, *Direito das Obrigações*, 2010, São Paulo, at 514–515, and DINIZ, *Curso de Direito Civil Brasileiro, Responsabilidade Civil*, 2010, São Paulo, at 528–529.
129. *See* CAVALIERI FILHO, *Programa de Responsabilidade Civil*, 2012, São Paulo, at 191 and 212.

Chapter 1. Vicarious Liability

108. In vicarious liability or liability for acts of others *stricto sensu*, as the main Brazilian author in torts, José de Aguiar Dias,[130] highlights, the grounds of the liability lie "in the fact of that certain people have the duty to oversee the behavior of others, whose inexperience or malice can cause harm to third parties;" it is "the duty of surveillance imputable to a person that renders him liable." This thus brings into being a complex relation, with the existence of two passive subjects, liable for victim's rights and therefore involving the payment of damages: on the one hand, the agent who carried out the act prejudicial to another's right, the *"de facto* author" of the harm; on the other hand, the agent liable in equity for the acts carried out by the de facto agent. In fact, the act carried out by the de facto agent creates an immediate causation, the mediate causation being a violation of the duty of oversight legally established to specific people, this being the legal basis of the liability for the acts of others.[131]

109. In Brazil, during the rule of the now revoked Civil Code of 1916, there was an intense scholarly and jurisprudential debate about the relationship of the legally liable agent to the de facto agent's acts in relation to the victim, regarding whether it should be considered subjective emerging from the notion of the presumption of guilt/negligence or whether it should be considered the subject of strict liability based on the risk theory. The promulgation of the New Civil Code of 2002 has ended the controversy, establishing in its Articles 932 and 933 strict liability in the cases described.[132] However, the Code brings in here the concept of strict secondary liability, since that is necessary for the concurrency of the two liability systems: the legally liable agent, under strict liability, and the liability of the de facto agent arising from his/her negligence. Both, however, are jointly liable towards the victim, in accordance with Article 942, sole paragraph of the Civil Code of 2002.[133]

110. In the current Brazilian torts system,[134] there are many situations of vicarious liability or liability for the acts of others *stricto sensu*, which are regulated under Articles 932 and 933 of the Civil Code of 2002: the strict liability of parents for damage caused by their underage children, set out Article 932, I; the strict liability of the tutor and curator for damage caused by their pupils and those in their care, set out by Article 932, II; the strict liability of employers for the harm caused by employees, servants and agents, set out by Article 932, III; the strict liability of hotels, bed and breakfasts, houses or establishments where one can find shelter for money for the harm caused by their guests, tenants and students, set out by Article 932, IV; and the strict liability of one who freely has participated in a crime up to the quantity for which he/she is liable for the damage caused by the criminals, set

---

130. *See* DIAS, *Da Responsabilidade Civil*, 2006, Rio de Janeiro, at 742–743.
131. *See* LIMA, *A responsabilidade civil pelo fato de outrem*, 1972, Rio de Janeiro, at 20.
132. *See* PEREIRA, *Responsabilidade Civil*, 2012, Rio de Janeiro, at 122–124.
133. *See* CAVALIERI FILHO, *Programa de Responsabilidade Civil*, 2012, São Paulo, at 193–194.
134. *See* Part III. Forms of Strict Liability, Ch. 5. Others.

out in Article 932, V. Furthermore, Articles 1.175 and 1.178 of the Civil Code establish the liability of a firm for the acts of its branches.

§1. EMPLOYEE/EMPLOYER

111. In Article 932, III, combined with Article 933, both from the Civil Code of 2002, is set out the strict liability of employers for the harm caused by their employees or servants, in the exercise of their jobs or by their jobs. This liability is based on the substitution theory, in which the employer, by ordering the services of the employee, is taking advantage of an instrument to allow him to carry out multiple tasks for the firm, extending his own activity, or based on the profit risk, where the employer benefits from the results of the activity carried by his employee, and therefore, assumes the risks arising from it. The employer's strict liability for the harm caused by his employees presupposes the existence of a legal contractual bond from which results the duty of the employer to take responsibility for the actions of an employee or anyone who provides service activities to third parties on his behalf.[135]

112. In the specification of the command contained in Article 932, III, of the Civil Code, are revealed the important concepts of employer and employee which are expressly pronounced in the CLT (1).[136] An employer is considered as "the individual or collective firm, which, assuming the risks of the economic activity, admits, pays wages and directs the personal performance of services;" considered equal to employers for the effects of job relations are "liberal professionals, charities, the dominical associations or not-for-profit institutions which may admit workers as employees" (Article 2, caput and paragraph first, of the CLT). "Any person who performs services of a non-final nature for the employer, under dependence on him and for wages in return" is considered an employee (Article 3 of the CLT).

113. The existence of a dependence relation or subordination between employer and employee is fundamental for the application of Article 932, III, of the Civil Code. Thus if the illicit or negligent act was carried out by the employee in the exercise of a typical activity ordered by the employer, it will be characterized by secondary strict liability of the employer for the harm caused to third parties. The notion of work normality is thus also relevant; this implies that the harmful act carried out by the employee has a temporal and local connection to acts carried out according to the employer's orders.[137]

114. The characterization of the employer's strict liability for the acts of his/hers employees is given by the demonstration of: (a) the practice of an illicit act by the employee based on intention or fault; (b) the existence of a harm caused to a third

---

135. *See* DIAS, *Da Responsabilidade Civil*, 2006, Rio de Janeiro, at 761–762, and CAVALIERI FILHO, *Programa de Responsabilidade Civil*, 2012, São Paulo, at 200–203.
136. Decree-Law n. 5.452, of May 1, 1943.
137. *See* STOCO, *Tratado de Responsabilidade Civil*, 2014, São Paulo, at 1285–1286 and 1289–1290, and GONÇALVES, *Responsabilidade Civil*, 2006, São Paulo, at 145–146.

party, which derives from an illicit act carried out by the employee; (c) the existence of a dependent or subordination relationship between the employee and the employer; (d) the fact that the employee has committed an illicit act in the exercise of his/her functions.[138] The extinction of employer's obligation to pay for the damages by proving that the harmful act was carried out outside the employee's orders is admitted. Furthermore, in these cases breaks in liability may apply such as legitimate defense, the strict performance of right and the destruction or harm to another's belongings for the removal of imminent harm are applicable (Article 188 of the Civil Code); the causation link may break due to act of God, chance, another's actions or the victim's exclusive negligence (concepts constructed by doctrine and jurisprudence); and there may be a reduction of damages by contributory negligence (Article 945 of the Civil Code).[139]

115. Brazilian jurisprudence on employer's liability for harm caused by employees or servants is vast, ranging from the most common cases such as: traffic accidents caused by the employee driving a company's car;[140] physical injury/death caused by an employee;[141] and moral harms caused by an employee linked to illicit conduct performed in the workplace, such as mobbing/bullying, sexual harassment and gender, race and religious prejudice.[142]

§2. Independent Contractors

116. In Article 932, III, combined with Article 933, both from the Civil Code, is set out the secondary strict liability of the principal for damages caused by its agent. The principal is "a person who charges another to buy, sell or practice any other act under his/her orders by his/her account, for some remuneration, named commission," and the agent is "any person hired to carry out material acts on account of the principal."[143] The establishment of a functional relationship, either permanent or temporary, between the principal and agent is essential for the characterization of the agency relation, the acts carried out by the agent being performed under the direction of and for the profit of the principal.[144]

117. Many contractual relationships can be framed as agency relationships for the appliance of secondary strict liability according to the terms of the Article 932,

---

138. *See* DINIZ, *Curso de Direito Civil Brasileiro, Responsabilidade Civil,* 2009, São Paulo, at 539–540.
139. *See* CAVALIERI FILHO, *Programa de Responsabilidade Civil,* 2012, São Paulo, at 203–204.
140. *See* STJ, 4ª Turma, REsp n° 1135988-SP, Relator Ministro Luis Felipe Salomão, DJe Oct. 17, 2013. Brasília.
141. *See* STJ, 3ª Turma, AgRg no AREsp n° 315871-MT, Relator Ministro Sidnei Beneti, DJe Jun. 21, 2013. Brasília.
142. *See* TST, 6ª Turma, AIRR n° 1203-74.2012.5.02.0008, Relator Ministro Augusto César Leite de Carvalho, DEJT 14.11.2014; TST, 3ª Turma, AIRR n° 1211-34.2013.5.03.0058, Relator Ministro Maurício Godinho Delgado, DEJT 22.05.2015; TST, 5ª Turma, RR – 831-24.2012.5.09.0011, Relator Ministro Emmanoel Pereira, DEJT 15.05.2015. Brasília.
143. *See* SILVA, *Vocabulário Jurídico,* 2008, Rio de Janeiro, at 184.
144. *See* WALD, *Obrigações e Contratos,* 2009, São Paulo, at 380.

III, of the Civil Code, such as: a mandate contract (Article 653 of the Civil Code, "whenever a person receives from other powers to carry out acts or manage interests in their name"); the commission contract (Article 693 of the Civil Code, "the contract of commission has as its object the acquisition or selling of goods by the commissionaire in his own name for the commitment"); the agency/distribution contract (Article 710 of the Civil Code, "by agency contracts, a person takes on, in a non-final character … the obligation to promote, for the other, for compensation, the fulfillment of certain business, in a determined zone, characterizing the area of distribution, when the agent has in his/her power the thing to be negotiated"), and; the business agency contract (Article 722 of the Civil Code, "through the business agency contract, one who is not bound to another through mandate, services or any other dependence relationship of any kind obliges himself/herself to another or several businesses, according to the received instructions").

118. On the other hand, the theme of independent contractors has given rise to many controversies among other relationships, such as services relations (Article 593 and following of the Civil Code) and in contractual relationships of travel (Article 610 and following of the Civil Code).[145] The lack of a labor or agency relation, in theory, does not authorize the appliance of secondary strict liability of Article 932, III, of the Civil Code, in these contractual relationships. However, a tendency by the jurisprudence to apply agency relations to them must be noted. The STJ has stated that "a typical labor contract is not necessary; a dependence relationship or the fact that one person performs services for the interest or on the orders of another is sufficient."[146] The secondary strict liability of the principal for the acts of his/her agents is used in such situations as: failure in the service performance of a doctor who is part of a clinical body of an hospital;[147] a traffic accident caused by a driver employed by the vehicle's owner,[148] and illicit acts carried out by a priest or other members who are a part of a religious institution.[149]

§3. LIABILITY OF LEGAL ENTITIES FOR ACTS OF THEIR ORGANS

119. Unlike the situation under the other hypotheses of vicarious liability or liability for the acts of others in a strict sense, regulated by the Civil Code in the Book I – the Law of Obligation, Articles 932 and 933, a firm's liability for the acts of its organs is regulated by the Book II – Firm Law, in Articles 1.175 and 1.178 of

---

145. *See,* GONÇALVES, *Responsabilidade Civil,* 2006, São Paulo, at 147.
146. *See* STJ, 4ª Turma, AgRg no REsp 1020237-MG, Relator Mininstro Luis Felipe Salomão, DJe 29.06.2012. Brasília.
147. *See* STJ, 3ª Turma, AgRg no Ag nº 1402439-RS, Relator Ministro Paulo de Tarso Sanseverino, DJe 10.04.2012. Brasília.
148. *See* STJ, 4ª Turma, AgRg no AREsp nº 287935-SP Relator Ministro Luis Felipe Salomão, DJe 27.05.2014. Brasília.
149. *See* STJ, 3ª Turma, REsp 1393699-PR, Relatora Ministra Nancy Andrighi, DJe 24.02.2014. Brasília.

the Civil Code. In the terms of Article 1.175, a firm is responsible for the acts carried out by its manager, for he/she is considered "the permanent agent in the exercise of the firm, in its headquarters, office, branch or agency" (Article 1.172); the manager's functions are to organize the direction of labor in one of these establishments, exercising a managerial role in the organization of the firm's structure. In addition, in the terms of Article 1.178 caput, a firm is liable for the acts carried out by any agent "carried out in its establishments related to the firm's activities, even those that are not formally authorized;" however, in the terms of Article 1.178, "when such acts are carried out outside the establishment, the principal will only be bound by acts performed within the limits of the powers given in writing." Therefore, an entrepreneur, legal or natural person, is liable for the acts of any his/her agents, the nature of the obligational bond between them being irrelevant, since they are carried out within the firm's establishment and are related to the firm's activities, even if their performance was not expressly and formally authorized. However, the entrepreneur will only be responsible for the business acts carried out by an agent outside the establishment within the limits of the powers given to the agent in written documents.[150]

---

150. *See* CAMPINHO, *O Direito da Empresa à luz no Novo Código Civil*, 2010, Rio de Janeiro, at 373.

Chapter 2. Liability of Parents, Teachers and Instructors (For Children, Minors, and Students)

120. In Article 932, I, combined with Article 933, both from the Civil Code, the secondary liability of parents for harm caused by acts performed by their underage children under their authority and supervision is laid down. The source of this liability lies in the legal duty of oversight of parents regarding their children, which spins off from the family authority established in Article 1.630 and following of the Civil Code, which imposes on parents many obligations, along with the duty to assist their children materially and morally and to supervise and guide them.[151]

121. In the application of Article 932, I of the Civil Code, along with the traditional elements of civil liability towards others, it is necessary to combine two specific elements, such as the fact that the children are underage, and the factual circumstance by which children are in their parents' care. If for a legal or legitimate reason, such as divorce or separation of the parents, adoption by another, or legal emancipation of the children by marriage, family authority can no longer be exercised, the parents are free from liability for harm occasioned by the acts of their underage children.[152] On the other hand, parents are not free from liability in the case of the voluntary emancipation of the children,[153] if the children are not living with their parents,[154] or if the children are outside their parents' living environment and no legal or legitimate reason removes the parents' duty of supervision.[155] Brazilian jurisprudence has recognized the secondary strict liability of parents for damages caused by the acts of their underage children in many situations, the most common being bodily injury or death caused by traffic[156] or caused by a gun fired by an underage person.[157]

122. In Article 932, II, combined with Article 933, both from the Civil Code, is laid down the secondary strict liability of the tutor and caretaker for the harms caused by those tutored and under the authority and supervision of a caretaker. The source of this liability lies in the legal duty of care of the tutor, who legally represents the underage children when their parents are deceased, have disappeared, or no longer have family authority, as laid down in Article 1.728 and following of the Civil Code; and in the supervisory duty of the caretaker, who legally represents underage persons who are incapable by reason of infirmity, mental illness, madness,

151. *See* CAVALIERI FILHO, *Programa de Responsabilidade Civil*, 2012, São Paulo, at 195.
152. *See* PEREIRA, *Responsabilidade Civil*, 2012, Rio de Janeiro, at 125–126.
153. *See* STJ, 4ª Turma, AgRg no Ag 1239557-RJ, Relator Ministra Maria Isabel Gallotti, DJe 17.10.2012. Brasília.
154. *See* STJ, 3ª Turma, AgRg no AREsp 220930-MG, Relator Mininstro Sidnei Beneti, DJe 29.10.2012. Brasília.
155. *See* PEREIRA, Responsabilidade Civil, 2012, Rio de Janeiro, at 127.
156. *See* STJ, 4ª Turma, REsp 1074937-MA, Relator Mininstro Luis Felipe Salomão, DJe 19.10.2009. Brasília.
157. *See* STJ, 3ª Turma, REsp 777327-RS, Relator Mininstro Massami Uyeda, DJe 01.12.2009. Brasília.

deafness, drug addiction or the prodigality of the caretaker, as set out in Article 1.767 and following of the Civil Code.[158]

123. The tutor's and caretaker's situation is very much akin to that of the parents: they are responsible for the acts carried out by those they tutor and care for on the same legal conditions as parents are for their children. Therefore, in general, the same principles that are applied to parents are applied to tutors and caretakers. The only relevant distinction in this matter is the right of redress, which, in the terms of Article 934 of the Civil Code, is possible for tutors and caretakers and forbidden to parents. The tort rules for parents, tutors and caretakers are established in the caput and text of Article 928 of the Civil Code, which lays down the subsidiary and contributory liability of a private person, responsible for civil acts in relation to someone who is under his/her wardship: "incapable persons are responsible for the harms they may cause, if the people for responsible for them do not have the obligation to be so or do not have sufficient resources," the compensation "not being required if it would deprive those incapable or persons who depend on them of necessities."[159]

124. In Article 932, IV, combined with Article 933, both from the Civil Code, is laid down the secondary strict liability of hotels, bed and breakfasts, houses or establishments where housing is offered for money, even for educational purposes, for damage caused by their guests, inhabitants or students. This liability lies in the contractual duty of supervision of educational institutions, hotels and establishments of this kind, such as mental institutions, kindergartens, nursing homes, etc. regarding their students, guests and residents. It is fundamental to secondary strict liability of this kind that the establishment receives payment in money for the services provided, otherwise, free housing would be liable for negligence, according to Article 927, caput of the Civil Code.[160] As educational and housing institutions are also service providers, they are subject to the secondary strict liability rules of the Civil Code, as well as the strict liability laid down in Article 14 of the Consumer's Protection Code,[161] according to the unanimous reasoning of the STJ.[162]

125. Educational institutions are responsible for harms caused by the acts of their students, while they are acting as students, which means that they are responsible for their acts while they are on the grounds of the educational institution or outside it while under the supervision of their teachers and professors and other educators connected to the educational institution. The most frequent situations of this

---

158. *See* GONÇALVES, *Responsabilidade Civil*, 2006, São Paulo, at 142–143, and CAVALIERI FILHO, 2010, São Paulo, at 198–199.
159. *See* FARIAS, BRAGA NETTO and ROSENVALD, *Novo Tratado de Responsabilidade Civil*, 2015, São Paulo, at 611–615.
160. *See* NADER, *Curso de Direito Civil – Responsabilidade Civil*, Saraiva, 2014, São Paulo, at 178–179.
161. *See* Part III, Ch. 3. Liability for Service.
162. *See* STJ, 4ª Turma, REsp 762075-DF, Relator Minintro Luis Felipe Salomão, DJe 26.09.2009, and; STJ, 3ª Turma, REsp 1376460-RS, Relator Marco Aurélio Bellizze, DJe 30.09.2014. Brasilia.

kind are harms caused by students to the physical and moral integrity of other students. Less frequent, but also creating liability are harms caused by students to educators and other employees of educational institutions or to others.[163]

126. As for hotels and other such institutions, it can be stated that these are responsible for any harm caused by their guests, but only while they are guests, namely, in the grounds of the establishment or extended areas such as parking and pool areas. Within this category is harm caused to other guests, employees, and others.[164]

---

163. *See* GONÇALVES, Responsabilidade Civil, 2006, São Paulo, at 158–161.
164. *See* FARIAS, BRAGA NETTO and ROSENVALD, *Novo Tratado de Responsabilidade Civil*, 2015, São Paulo, at 629–631.

Chapter 3. Liability for Things and Animals

127. The Brazilian system of torts regulates liability for things and liability for animals in specific normative articles. The Civil Code sets out the liability for things in Article 937, such as harms caused by construction or buildings in ruin, and in Article 938, the harms caused by throwing things that have fallen from buildings. Liability for animals is set out in Article 936 of the Civil Code. In addition, by doctrinal and jurisprudential construction, the theory of a thing's supervision is applied, which widens the applicable spectrum of the duty of care to things or animals that are potentially harmful.

128. In terms of Article 937 of the Civil Code, "the owner of a building or construction is responsible for any harm that results from it being a ruin, if this results from a lack of necessary repairs." As a natural consequence of power exercised over a thing (Article 1.228 of the Civil Code), the owner of a building or construction should make the necessary repairs, not allowing them to fall into ruin and cause harm to third parties. The expression "ruin" is interpreted in a broad sense, including the concept of complete or partial destruction of the building, or its parts such as tiles, glass, marquees, insulating material, and other things. The expression "building" is also admitted in a broader sense, encompassing the construction of walls, bridges, bypasses, lampposts, channels, elevators, escalators, and other things.[165]

129. In terms of Article 938 of the Civil Code, "anyone who inhabits a building, or part of it, is responsible for the harm caused by things fallen or thrown from it in an inappropriate place." A person having the supervision or occupation of a building or part of it, either as its owner, renter, enjoyer, or bailee, is liable for the harms caused to others from things fallen or thrown from his/her building. The legal text can be extensively interpreted, encompassing not only housing, but also commercial buildings such as offices, stores, event centers, among others.[166] With regard to a horizontal or vertical condominium, it will be considered liable where it cannot be verified precisely where the object came from, according to the STJ;[167] the obligation to pay damages allocated to the condominium is an application of alternative causation.

130. As consolidated by the rationale of doctrine and jurisprudence, regarding Article 937 of Civil Code, liability for the total or partial ruin of the building (if the building itself falls down, totally or partially, or things that are part of the building

---

165. *See* NADER, *Curso de Direito Civil, Responsabilidade Civil*, 2014, Rio de Janeiro, at 199–201, and; DINIZ, *Curso de Direito Civil Brasileiro, Responsabilidade Civil*, 2009, São Paulo, at 558–559.

166. *See* NADER, *Curso de Direito Civil, Responsabilidade Civil*, 2014, Rio de Janeiro, at 206–207, and; STOCO, *Tratado de Responsabilidade Civil*, 2014, São Paulo, at 1304–1305.

167. *See* STJ, 4ª Turma, REsp 64.682-RJ, Relator Ministro Bueno de Souza, DJ 29.03.1999, p. 180. Brasília.

are detached from it), and Article 938 of the Civil Code, on the throwing or falling of things from buildings (objects that do not form part of the building, but have fallen or been thrown from it) constitute modalities of strict liability for things, as a consequence of risk theory. Therefore, only harm and the characterization of the cause are needed to originate an obligation to pay damages; any analysis of due diligence or due care of the ruin or the source of the fallen or thrown things by the building's owner is unnecessary. The defenses of force majeure, an act of God, third party and exclusive fault of the victim are admitted.[168]

131. In the terms of Article 936 of the Civil Code, "the owner or keeper of an animal will pay damages for any harm it causes, if the victim's own fault or an act of God are not proved." Usually, as a natural consequence of the power over a thing (Article 1.228 of the Civil Code), liability for animals falls on the owner, the person with command and control of the animal. However, the owner can transfer command and control of the animal to a third party, a situation where liability for animals will pass to the animal's current keeper. This is what happens, for instance, when the owner transfers the custody of a domestic animal to a clinic, hotel, or veterinary hospital, or when the owner transfers the custody of a horse to a stud farm or horse society. Therefore, the verification of who had the custody of the animal at the time when the event occurred is fundamental to the appliance of the legal hypothesis.[169] The legal text is applicable to domestic/tamed and wild animals in captivity such as, for example, in a circus or a zoo, and is not applicable to wild animals that are not legally possessed or owned.[170] Among the diverse hypotheses of application of the legal rule are injuries caused by savage dogs or wild animals kept in captivity; the destruction of crops or damage to property caused by domestic animals; and traffic accidents caused by animals wandering on to roads.[171]

132. According to the mainstream rationale found in doctrine and jurisprudence, Article 936 of Civil Code of 2002 establishes strict liability for animals, derived from risk theory; it is therefore sufficient to characterize the harm and a causal link between the animal's behavior and the harm for the obligation to pay damages to arise for the owner or custodian of the animal. Any question about the due diligence or care of the owner or custodian during their care of the animal is thus unnecessary.[172] By express legal disposition, the causation excludes acts of

---

168. *See* CAVALIERI FILHO, 2010, São Paulo, at 220, 234 and 236, and; STOCO, *Tratado de Responsabilidade Civil*, 2014, São Paulo, at 1301, 1307 and 1314.
169. *See* FARIAS, in: Rodrigues Junior, Mamede e Rocha, *Responsabilidade Civil Contemporânea*, 2011, São Paulo, at 207–208.
170. *See* CAVALIERI FILHO, *Programa de Responsabilidade Civil*, 2010, São Paulo, at 229.
171. *See* GONÇALVES, *Responsabilidade Civil*, 2006, São Paulo, at 278–282.
172. *See* CAVALIERI FILHO, *Programa de Responsabilidade Civil*, São Paulo, 2010, at 228–229; STOCO, *Tratado de Responsabilidade Civil*, São Paulo, 2015, at 1316–1317, and; SCHEREIBER, *Novos Paradigmas da Responsabilidade Civil*, São Paulo, 2009, at 32. On the other hand, assuming that the rule laid down in Art. 936 of the 2002 Civil Code is negligence with presumption of guilt, *see* NADER, *Curso de Direito Civil, Responsabilidade Civil*, Rio de Janeiro, 2014, at 189, and; DINIZ, *Curso de Direito Civil Brasileiro, Responsabilidade Civil*, São Paulo, 2009, at 551.

God and victims' exclusive own faults. Therefore, the owner or custodian of the animal can be freed of liability if it is proved that the harm arose from an unpredictable external fact or by the victim's own fault, for instance, if the victim provoked the animal or behaved unwisely towards it.[173]

173. *See* FARIAS, in: Rodrigues Junior, Mamede e Rocha, *Responsabilidade Civil Contemporânea*, 2011, São Paulo, at 209.

Part III. Forms of Strict Liability

133. The existence of a dualistic system of tort law represents a contemporary phenomenon, the basic rule of negligence, raised to the position of a general principle of liability, coexisting with the rule of strict liability, applicable in particular cases especially provided for in all legal systems.[174] Under the rule of negligence, the agent is responsible for illicit acts, which produces an obligation to pay damages arising from the guilt/negligence of the person who causes the harm. For the establishing of this obligation, the convergence of three elements is necessary: the negligent act, the harm and causation. Under the rule of strict liability, the obligation arises regardless of whether the agent was negligent or not, prescribed by a legal fact described in the normative system as a source of liability, along with the presence of harm and a causal relation.[175]

134. Considering the traditional legal doctrine, the application of strict liability is usually based on reasons such as the imperative of social politics, especially public order and social welfare; the standard terms of equity; the abuse of rights, characterized by the exercise of rights by an owner with a lack of respect for the economic and social goals which are the reason for that right having been instituted or using these rights to harm morals and good custom, or even to exceed the limits of good faith; the guarantee theory, built on the duty of care imposed on particular people such as parents for their children, employers for their employees; and, above all, risk theory.[176] Considering the theory of law and economics (models of unilateral and bilateral causation, analyzing factors such as level of care, level of activity, level of information, risk distribution, and administrative costs), along general lines, strict liability is established as an efficient mechanism of control of the level of risk activity carried out by the agent, since it induces the internalization of social costs and reduces the activity to the socially optimal level.[177]

---

174. *See* DAM, European Tort Law, 2006, Oxford, at 256; WERRO, PALMER e HAHN, Strict Liability in European Tort Law: an Introduction, in WERRO and PALMER, *The Boundaries of Strict Liability in European Tort Law*, 2004, Durham, at 473.
175. *See* PEREIRA, *Responsabilidade Civil*, 1998, Rio de Janeiro, at 35.
176. *See*, PAULA, *As excludentes de Responsabilidade Civil Objetiva*, São Paulo, 2007, at 16–30.
177. *See* SCHAEFFER, HAND-BERND and MÜLLER-LANGER, Strict Liability Versus Negligence, in: BOUCKAERT and DE GEEST, *Encyclopedia of Law and Economics*, 2009, Cheltenham, at 3–45; and, BATTESINI, *Direito e Economia, Novos Horizontes no Estudo da Responsabilidade Civil no Brasil*, 2011, São Paulo, at 125–182.

135. From a comparative perspective, it can be verified that contemporary tort systems all have strict liability rules, focusing on the harms caused rather than the agent's negligence, as occurs in environmental liability and the causation of damage in the liability of animals, transport liability, dangerous product liability and industrial liability.[178] In addition, according to the degree of participation of the judiciary in the application of strict liability, legal systems can be classified as: open systems, in which the task of defining the list of activities to apply strict liability is within the competence of the judiciary (a typical example is the United States); and closed systems, in which the definition of the list of activities is an attribution of the legislature, and where the judiciary is not allowed to qualify activities which incur strict liability (a typical example is Germany); and mixed systems, in which, in addition to applying strict liability to a list of activities prepared by the legislature, the judiciary has express legislative authorization to expand the list of activities (as is the case of Brazil).[179]

136. In many ways, the Brazilian tort law system follows the French civil law tradition. Brazil has a dualist system of liability, which combines the basic rule of negligence (Article 186 combined with Article 927, caput, of the Civil Code), with strict liability, focusing on the cause of the harm and the presence of the harm itself, regulated by specific statutes, by the Federal Constitution of 1988, and by the Civil Code of 2002. Following this rationale, the manifestations of two major Brazilian jurists, namely Caio Mário da Silva Pereira,[180] author of the Draft Code of Obligations, in reforming the Brazilian Civil Code of 1916, and Miguel Reale,[181] the General Coordinator of the Commission responsible for preparing the Brazilian Civil Code of 2002, are emblematic. Pereira highlights that the two regimes coexist: negligence represents the basic notion and the general principle of liability based on negligence and strict liability is applied in cases specified by law, or when the injury arises from a situation created by an operator, profession or activity which exposed the victim to the risk of harm. Miguel Reale states that "both forms of liability are intertwined and thereby make themselves dynamic;" thus it should be recognized that "negligence is the general rule, therefore the individual should be liable predominantly from his action or omission due to negligence or illicit will," which "does not exclude that the structure of a business may lead to strict liability; this is a fundamental point."

---

178. *See* KOCH & KOZIOL, Comparative Conclusions, in KOCH and KOZIOL, Unification of Tort Law: Strict Liability, 2002, The Hague, at 395–406.
179. *See* BATTESINI, Comparative Tort Law and Economics: Strict Liability in Brazilian Legal Practice, 2013, New York, SSRN, at 21, http://ssrn.com/abstract=2263506.
180. *See* PEREIRA, *Instituições de Direito Civil*, 2008, Rio de Janeiro, at 562–563.
181. *See* REALE, *Diretrizes Gerais sobre o Projeto de Código Civil*, in REALE, *Estudos de Filosofia e Ciência do Direito*, 1978, São Paulo, at 176–177.

Chapter 1. Road and Traffic Accidents

137. As occurs in the USA and UK,[182] the traffic law tort system in Brazil is based on negligence, set out in Article 186, combined with Article 927, caput, of the Civil Code. It is up to the victim to prove the negligence of the defendant, the harm caused and the causation that connects the harm and the defendant.[183] It is broadly speaking the theory of negligence versus the legality rule, which predicts that where an express legal or normative duty is ignored there is a presumption of negligence.[184] In this regard, the conduct and circulation norms set out by the Brazilian Traffic Code are of fundamental importance (Law no. 9,503/97); this acts as a standard of comparison for factually negligent behavior. In the case of traffic accidents the following defenses are applicable: legitimate self-defense, the regular exercise of a right, the destruction or harm of another's belongings or nuisance to avoid imminent harm (Article 188 of the Civil Code); the causation link break of chance, an act of God and third-party facts such as the victim's exclusive negligence; and the reduction of damages by contributory negligence.

138. The scope of Brazilian jurisprudence on traffic accidents is wide,[185] covering roads and street-level accidents, accidents between vehicles, vehicular damage to pedestrian and bicycle riders, accidents triggered by bad road conditions, by bad signing, by the presence of animals and objects on the pavement, mechanical failures, and mainly by the negligent/imprudent misconduct of drivers breaking traffic rules. Research has estimated that 98% of accidents are caused by the negligence/imprudence of drivers, the most common causes being excessive speed, use of cellphones while driving, drunk drivers and general disrespect for the rules of careful driving. Brazil has one of the highest death rates by traffic accidents in the world, 23.6 deaths per 100,000 persons (2012), 45,689 deaths – registered in 2012 and 31,945 deaths registered in 2019.[186] These data are alarming and have triggered discussions about the efficacy of public policies in accident prevention and, in the field of torts, have justified doctrinal positions that sustain the necessity of the use of strict liability in some situations,[187] either due to the direct application by the judiciary of the general clause of strict liability for risk activities stated in Article 927, of the current Civil Code or, as occurs in other civil law countries such as France and Germany, through specific legislation connected with mandatory insurance.[188]

---

182. *See* KOCH & KOZIOL, Comparative Conclusions, in KOCH and KOZIOL, Unification of Tort Law: Strict Liability, 2002, The Hague, at 399.
183. *See* COELHO, *Curso de Direito Civil – Responsabilidade Civil*, 2005, São Paulo, at 329.
184. *See* CAVALIERI FILHO, *Programa de Responsabilidade Civil*, 2012, São Paulo, at 43.
185. *See* STOCO, *Tratado de Responsabilidade Civil*, 2014, São Paulo, at 1887–2117.
186. *See* OBSERVATÓRIO NACIONAL DE SEGURANÇA VIÁRIA – ONSV, *Retrato da Segurança Viária no Brasil*, 2014. Brasília, disponível em http://onsv.org.br.
187. *See* BATTESINI, *Direito e Economia, Novos Horizontes no Estudo da Responsabilidade Civil no Brasil*, 2011, São Paulo, at 246–247.
188. *See* KOCH & KOZIOL, Comparative Conclusions, in KOCH and KOZIOL, Unification of Tort Law: Strict Liability, 2002, The Hague, at 400.

139. In fact, the presence of mandatory insurance for automobile vehicle owners (DPVAT), established by Law no. 6,194/74, is another characteristic of the Brazilian tort system in traffic accidents. In addition to the conventional voluntary insurance of civil liability, the vehicle owner, at the time of obtaining or renewing the vehicle's license, is obliged to acquire insurance in favor of third parties as potential accident victims. In fact, the risks related to the movement of vehicles are so extensive that the Brazilian legislator has established mandatory insurance, DPVAT, as a means to guarantee a minimum compensation to accident victims (hospital, death, or permanent invalidity condition expenses) regardless of whether the driver was negligent or not.

Chapter 2. Product Liability

140. Product liability in Brazil is regulated in the CDC, Law no. 8,078/90, among the general rules of the Civil Code of 2002. In giving content to Article 5, XXXII, of the Federal Constitution, the Brazilian legislator, showing the marked influence of Resolution 39/248, of April 9, 1985, of the General Assembly of the United Nations and the European Union Directives 84/450 and 85/374, of July 25, 1985,[189] has promulgated the CDC, in force since September 11, 1990. In the elucidating expression of Sérgio Cavalieri Filho,[190] the CDC has created a "super multidisciplinary legal structure, legal norms applicable to all law branches where there are consumer relations." In addition to this wide field of application, the CDC is known for being a law codified through principles and general clauses, which evokes the principles of strict good faith (Article 4, III), prevention (Article 6, VI), full compensation (Article 6, VI), information (Article 6, III), and the rule of law (Article 12, paragraph 1). Another notable characteristic of the Code is the fact that it concentrates on the notion of consumer relations and circulation of products (Article 3, paragraph 1) and services (Article 3, paragraph 2), establishing regulatory norms of general application, specific to the circulation of products and services.[191]

141. In essence, civil liability in consumer relations occurs either when a product is brought to the market and is defective in the hands of the final consumer or when a product causes harm to the consumer. This is a contractual or extra-contractual legal relation that has on the one side the supplier and on the other the consumer who is the object of the circulation of products or services. The CDC defines the basic concepts of supplier, consumer, product and service. The legal definition of supplier is very wide, including all participants in the productive-distributive cycle. A supplier is "a physical or legal person, public or private, national or foreigner, as well as non-personal entities that are involved in the production, assembly, importation, exportation, distribution or commercialization of products or services performance" (Article 3). The legal definition of a consumer has as a structuring element the notion of the final destination of the product, "every physical or legal person who/which acquires a product or service as final destination" being considered as a "consumer" (Article 2). The STJ[192] has consolidated the rationale in the sense that no consumer relation is involved in the acquisition of goods or services by a natural or legal person whose goal is to implement or expand his core business, rejecting, therefore, the idea of the existence of a simple consumption act as sufficient, independent of its finality. In addition to the direct consumer, the CDC also applies to the indirect consumer or consumer by extension, defined as "the collectivity of people, even those who cannot be determined, who

---

189. *See* BENJAMIN, *Código de Defesa do Consumidor*, 2011, São Paulo, at 1–8.
190. *See* CAVALIERI FILHO, *Programa de Responsabilidade Civil*, 2012, São Paulo, at 485–486.
191. The common regulatory rules and the specific rules of the circulation of products will be considered in this chapter and the specific regulatory rules for services circulation will be considered in the next chapter.
192. *See* STJ, 2ª Seção, REsp 541867-BA, Relator Ministro Antônio de Pádua Ribeiro, DJ 16.05.2005 p. 227. Brasília.

have interacted in consumer relations" (Article 2, single paragraph). Products or services are the object of express legal definition. According to the CDC, "any good, mobile or immobile, material or immaterial" (Article 3, paragraph 1) can be considered a product and services are "any activity offered on the consumer market, for remuneration" (Article 3, paragraph 2).

142. The CDC adopts a system, which, *lato sensu*, works with two categories of defective products or services, distinguishing product defects from product accidents. Product defects are the result of less harmful misassembly which affects the quality or quantity of products or services and makes them inadequate or inappropriate for consumption or which could diminish their value, such as disparities between the container, label, packaging, or publicity indications and their content/performance (Article 18, caput and Article 20, caput). Product or services accidents are major defects that compromise product safety and may cause harm to the consumer (Article 12, caput, and Article 14, caput). Both emerge from a defect in the product or service, though while in the defects stated by the CDC the harm is restricted to the product or service itself which leads to the malfunction, misuse or fruition and dysfunction, in a product or services accident, the defect is so severe that it may cause external harm, which may affect the consumer or third parties and cause the consumer and/or others material or extra-material harm.[193] The solution adopted by the legislator for a product or services defect implies the obligation of the supplier to make good the defect or replace the product/re-execute the service or finally to restitute the cost of the product to the consumer, or to proportionally discount the price of the product according to the consumer's wish (Article 18, paragraph 1, I, II, and III, and Article 20, caput, I, II, and III). For a product or services accident *stricto sensu*, the legislator has instigated a more severe regime, combining tort law rules to repair the harm caused to the consumer and/or others due to the consumer accident.

143. Supplier liability for product defects or facts *stricto sensu* is given by strict liability, which means that the supplier is responsible regardless of the existence or not of negligent/diligent behavior for the harm caused to consumers or others by the release of the defective product on to the market. According to the CDC, "the manufacturer, the producer, the constructor, national or foreign is responsible, independently of fault, for the reparation of the harm caused to consumers, arising from defects in the design, manufacturing, construction, assembly, formulas, manipulation, presentation or storage of their products, as well as information that may be insufficient or inadequate regarding their use or risks" (Article 12, caput). The strict liability of the production chain is joined. According to the CDC, the manufacturer, the producer, the constructor and the importer are responsible jointly for the release of the defective product on the market (Article 7, paragraph, Article 18, caput, and Article 25, paragraphs 1 and 2). The strict liability of the merchant for the release of the defective product, in turn, is subsidiary, which means that the merchant is responsible to the consumer when the manufacturer, constructor, producer or importer cannot be identified or when perishable products are not properly stored

---

193. *See* CAVALIERI FILHO, *Programa de Responsabilidade Civil*, 2012, São Paulo, at 488.

by the merchant himself (Article 13). The party held liable by the consumer has a right of redress against the other participants in the industrial or service generation chain (Article 13, paragraph). The jurisprudence of the STJ has consolidated the sense that the consumer can, by his own choice, exercise his claim against the supplier of the product or service that is most convenient to him/her.[194]

144. For the application of strict liability of suppliers by accident or defect of product or services *stricto sensu*, the CDC considers a product defective if it "does not offer the safety that is legitimately expected of it," taking into account the relevant circumstances, namely: the product presentation (e.g., lack of user manual, medical leaflet, inadequate packaging, etc.); the use and risks that are reasonably to be expected (non-compliance with a reasonable expectation of the consumer); and the time (available technology) at which the product was released (Article 12, paragraph 1, I–III). According to the CDC (Article 12, caput), product defects may be of conception (design, creation, formula), production (construction, assembly, manipulation, manufacturing) or of market release (publicity, information, presentation, or storage). A product is not considered defective by the mere fact of another product of better quality being put on the market (Article 12, paragraph 2). In addition to the defect of product or service released to the market, the strict liability of the supplier in consumer accidents presupposes a causation nexus, the existence of material or immaterial harm caused to the consumer. The theme of the quantification of moral harm in consumer accidents has triggered doctrinal and jurisprudential controversy, stemming from the legislator's choice not to establish a maximum or minimum limitation or to fix standard values for this kind of harm.[195]

145. The CDC also sets out liability exclusion clauses for the supplier of a defective product or service, by excluding causation; for instance, by the supplier proving that he did not release the product on to the market, that the defect does not exist, or that the fault is exclusive to the consumer or a third party (Article 12, paragraph 3, I–III). The CDC also sets out causation excluding factors for product accident liability such as proof of the non-existence of a defect, the victim's exclusive fault or a third party's exclusive fault (Article 14, paragraph 3, I and II). The application of chance, acts of God and development risk to consumer accidents are not mentioned in the CDC, which has brought about the doctrinal and jurisprudential controversy,[196] the STJ being in favor of applying these causality-excluding factors.[197] Regarding products or services that are risky by nature, quality or function (weapons, medicines with high-risk rate, medicines with contraindications, agrotoxics, etc.), there is no illicit conduct on the part of the supplier who releases them on to the market provided the duty to give adequate information established in Article 9 of the CDC is observed: "the supplier of products or services that are potentially harmful or dangerous to health or safety should offer information in an

---

194. *See* STJ, 3ª Turma, REsp nº 554.876-RJ, Relator Ministro Carlos Alberto Menezes Direito. Brasília.
195. *See* STOCO, *Tratado de Responsabilidade Civil*, 2014, São Paulo, at 634–635.
196. *See Ibid.*, at 616–617 and 624.
197. *See* STJ, 3ª Turma, REsp nº 120.647/SP, Relator Ministro Eduardo Ribeiro, DJ 15.05.2000, p. 156. Brasília.

obvious and adequate manner about the harmfulness or danger." The reduction of damages for contributory liability in consumer accidents is another source of controversy between doctrine and jurisprudence,[198] the STJ being in favor of the application of this institute, as stated in Article 945 of the Civil Code.[199]

146. Agreeing and complementing the strict liability of the supplier of products for accidents or defects in the CDC, the Civil Code of 2002 has embodied in analogous fashion the strict liability of individual entrepreneurs and firms for harm caused by their products in circulation, stating that "apart from other cases set out in special laws, individual entrepreneurs and firms are responsible whether at fault or not for the harms caused by their products in circulation" (Article 931, of the Civil Code). This is a general clause of strict liability even wider than that laid down in the CDC (Article 12); thus the statement in the Civil Code is applicable even when there is no consumer relation, therefore encompassing a wider spectrum of accidents caused by defective products.[200]

147. In addition to the rules of civil liability of the supplier, the CDC lays down instruments that are complementary in a situation of risk of consumer accidents and in defense of the consumer. In the Administrative Code (Article 56, I–XII) and the Criminal Code (Articles 63–74) sanctions are also laid down. They also set out the disregard of legal entity for firms that act against consumers, abuse their rights, violate the law and statutes of the social contract, go bankrupt, are insolvent or shut down their activities due to bad administration (Article 28). The defense of the interests of consumers and victims can be exercised individually or collectively (Article 81). A collective defense will be exercised when it is a case of the interests of diffuse rights (trans-individuals, the indivisible nature of a group, category, or class of persons) and individual rights that are homogeneous (of common origin); such a defense can be put forward by a public ministry, the Federal Union, the estates, municipalities, the Federal District, and entities and branches of the public administration (Article 81, paragraph, I–III, and Article 82, I–IV).

198. *See* CAVALIERI FILHO, *Programa de Responsabilidade Civil*, 2012, São Paulo, at 500.
199. STJ, 4ª Turma, REsp n° 287.849-SP, Relator Ministro Ruy Rosado do Aguiar, DJ 13.08.2001, p. 165. Brasília.
200. *See* FACCHINI NETO, *A Responsabilidade Civil no Novo Código, Revista do Tribunal Superior do Trabalho*, RS, v. 76, n. 1, p. 17–63, January/March 2010, Porto Alegre, at 196.

Chapter 3. Liability for Services

148. The application field of the CDC is wide in matters of services, including, by express legal disposition, "any activity supplied on the consumer market, for remuneration, including banking, financial, credit and insurance activities, apart from those of a labor nature" (Article 3, paragraph 2). The STJ has consolidated the rationale that the CDC is applicable to financial institutions,[201] private retirement entities[202] and health insurance contracts.[203] Public services, including water supply, electric supply, gas supply, telephone services and public transportation, by express legal disposition also are subject to the CDC (Article 22, caput and paragraph).

149. Supplier liability for accidents or defects of products or services *stricto sensu* is objective, which means that the supplier is responsible independently of fault for the harm caused to consumers by defective services released onto the market. According to the CDC, "the supplier of services is responsible, independently of the existence of fault, for the compensation of harm caused to consumers by defects related to services performance, as well as for insufficient or inadequate information about their use and risks" (Article 14, caput). The strict liability of participants in the generation of services chain, including merchants, for the release of the defective service onto the market is a case of joint liability, the right of redress being secured to the consumer, who can take action against whichever supplier is more convenient to him/her. In order to apply the strict liability of the supplier for the fact or defect of service *stricto sensu*, the CDC considers a service defective if it "does not supply the security that the consumer could expect taking into consideration the relevant circumstances," including the method of supply and the result and risks that may be reasonably expected at the time of its release (Article 14, paragraph 1, I–III). A service is not considered as defective simply because of the subsequent adoption of new techniques by the market (Article 14, paragraph 2).

150. Complementing the rule of strict liability of the supplier for the service accident or defect *stricto sensu* present in the CDC, the Civil Code states the strict liability of the transporter for harm or damage caused to persons and luggage,[204] establishing the "voidance of any clause that may exclude liability" (Article 734, caput, of the Civil Code).

151. In its system of strict liability of the supplier for the service accident or defect in the strict sense, the CDC makes an exception for professionals, whose liability is subjective. By express legal provision, "the responsibility of independent professionals shall be determined upon verification of guilt" (Article 14, paragraph 4). Therefore, considering the *natura intuitu personae* of the service provided by

---

201. *See* STJ, *súmula* 297. Brasilia.
202. *See* STJ, *súmula* 321. Brasilia.
203. *See* STJ, *súmula* 469. Brasilia.
204. *See* STJ, 3ª Turma, AgRg no Ag n° 778.804/RJ, Relator Ministro Humberto Gomes de Barros, DJe 14.12.2007. Brasília.

liberal professions, the Brazilian legislator has opted for the subjective responsibility of doctors, lawyers, engineers, dentists and other professionals,[205] making it necessary to ascertain fault, in line with Article 186 combined with Article 927, caput, of the Civil Code of 2002.[206]

---

205. *See* Part I, Ch. 2, §1. Liability of Professionals.
206. In addition to the specific rules on the circulation of services covered in this chapter, *see* the common regulatory rules of the circulation of goods and services, dealt with in the previous chapter.

Chapter 4. Environmental Liability

152. The preservation of the environment is a fundamental value in Brazilian society; it is even protected as a constitutional value (Article 170, VI of the Brazilian Federal Constitution). The Federal Constitution of 1988 establishes an ecologically balanced environment as "of common use of the people, essential to the healthy quality of life, binding public authorities and the collectivity with the duty to defend and preserve it for present and future generations" (Article 225, caput). The constitutional text itself sets out a bundle of measures for public authorities intended to secure the preservation of the environment (Article 225, paragraph 1, I–VII), stating three spheres of sanctions for anyone who harms the environment, namely: criminal, administrative and civil sanctions (Article 225, paragraph 3). In this respect, the Federal Constitution of 1988 has incorporated Law no. 6,938/81, the legal statement which established the National Defense of the Environment Policy, which contains rules of civil liability in environmental law, into the Constitution itself.

153. The National Policy of Environment Defense Law (*Lei de Política Nacional de Defesa do Meio Ambiente*) has internalized the polluter pays principle of ECO92, as an instrument of control of the level of risk to the environment of an activity and the internalization of negative externalities of a firm or activity. It also internalizes the precautionary principle as an instrument to deter environmental damage, when there is no scientific proof that there is any meaningful harm to the environment arising from a particular activity, and the precautionary principle is a means of strict liability connected to environmental damages where there is a probability of harm. As stated the Article 14, paragraph 1, of Law no. 6,938/81, the polluter is "obliged, regardless of his negligence/diligence to pay damages to the environment and to third parties affected by his/her activity." The adoption of strict liability removes the fault/negligence content of the discussion of the nature of the activity, although it does not remove the necessity of proof of the other two conditions of civil liability, namely, the causation nexus and the harm, though it may bring about disputes in terms of doctrine and jurisprudence in the application of the precautionary principle.

154. The doctrine[207] and the jurisprudence[208] at large justify strict liability in environmental damages through the integral risk theory, an extreme modality of risk theory which allows the flexibility of the causation nexus burden of proof with the adoption of the theory of antecedent equivalence instead of adequate causation, as a means to extend the agents who are liable for the compensation of environmental harm. In addition, integral risk theory, as adopted by the STJ, can find that there is no causation nexus in the case of factors such as acts of God, third-party accidents

---

207. *See* PAULA, *As excludentes de Responsabilidade Civil Objetiva*, 2007, São Paulo, at 75.
208. *See* STJ, 2ª Seção, REsp nº 1.354.536/SE, Relator Ministro Luis Felipe Salomão, DJe 05.05.2014. Brasília.

and exclusive victim fault.[209] The theme of collective moral harm in doctrine[210] and jurisprudence[211] is polarized between those who defend and those who reject its application to environmental law.

---

209. *See* STJ, 3ª Turma, AgRg no REsp nº 1.412.664/SP, Relator Ministro Raul Araújo, DJe 11.03.2014. Brasília.
210. *See* STOCO, Tratado de Responsabilidade Civil, 2014, São Paulo, at 1182–1188.
211. *See* STJ, 2ª Turma, REsp 1.328.753/MG, Relator Herman Benjamin, DJe. 28.05.2013, and, STJ, 1ª Turma, REsp. 598.281/MG, Relator Ministro Teori Albino Zavaski, DJe 01.06.2006. Brasília.

Chapter 5. Others

155. In addition to the circumstances analyzed in the previous chapters, strict liability in Brazil is established by specific statutes, along with the Constitution of 1988 and the Civil Code of 2002. The first law to state strict liability in Brazil is the Executive Act no. 2,681, of December 7, 1912, which regulated railroad transportation, according to activity risk theory, in its Article 26, and made "the railroads liable for every harm that the exploration of their lines caused to marginal owners."[212] Exclusions from liability specific to railroads is established in the text of Article 26: "the liability will cease, however, if the harmful event arises from a direct cause of infraction by the owner of a statute or regulation related to buildings, plantations, excavations, material storage or care of animals at the side of railroads."

156. In the Mining Code (Executive Law Act no. 227, February 28, 1967) lies another cause of strict liability in Article 47, VIII, in which the owner of a concession of a mining operation is responsible for the "harms and losses to third parties that result directly or indirectly from the exploration." The damages caused by mining activity are, in essence environmental, for which the rules are set out in the prior chapter.

157. Strict liability is also laid down in the Brazilian Aeronautics Code (*Código Brasileiro de Aeronáutica*, Law no. 7,565, December 19, 1986), which, in its Article 268, makes the air transportation explorer liable for "damage to third parties on the surface, caused directly by flight or manoeuvring by a person or thing falling or projected by it." The exclusion of liability specific to air transportation is established in Article 268, paragraph 2, I–IV; it includes the lack of a direct cause and effect relation between the harm and the facts arising; the fact of the harm resulting from the passage of the flight through the airspace while complying with the rules of air traffic; if the flight is operated by a third party or agent, or another dependent who has exercised reasonable caution and if exclusive victim fault is found.

158. With the advent of the General Personal Data Protection Law, Law no. 13,709, August 14, 2018, Articles 42–45, which establish the rules regarding the civil liability of personal data-processing agents, the doctrinal debate on the nature of the obligation to indemnify began, either subjective (negligence), based on the lack of a duty of conduct imposed on the treating agent, or objective (strict liability) based on the risk of the activity carried out by the agents. This is a controversial issue, which will be defined by jurisprudential construction in the coming years.[213]

---

212. The force of Executive Act no. 2.681, Dec. 7, 1912, in the face of the promulgation of the CDC and the Civil Code of 2002, is under discussion. *See* CAVALIERI FILHO, *Programa de Responsabilidade Civil*, 2012, São Paulo, at 147, and, DIAS, *Da Responsabilidade Civil*, 2006, Rio de Janeiro, at 597.
213. *See* MULHOLLAND, Caitlin, *A LGPD e o fundamento da responsabilidade civil dos agentes de tratamento de dados pessoais: culpa ou risco?*. Available at https://www.migalhas.com.br/coluna/migalhas-de-responsabilidade-civil/329909/a-lgpd-e-o-fundamento-da-responsabilidade-civil-dos-agentes-de-tratamento-de-dados-pessoais--culpa-ou-risco.

159. The Federal Constitution of 1988 determines the exploration of nuclear services and installations of any nature to be within the competence of the Federal Union, establishing in its Article 21, XXIII, "d," that "civil liability for nuclear harm does not depend on the existence of fault." Strict liability in nuclear activities is also regulated by Law no. 6,453, of October 17, 1977, which in Article 4, I–III, establishes that the nuclear installation is responsible independent of fault for the reparation of nuclear harm occurring in the installation or provoked by material of nuclear origin or sent to the installation. The liability excluding factors specific to nuclear activities are established in Articles 6 and 8 of Law no. 6,453, namely that the damage is the victim's exclusive fault; and that the damage may be caused directly by armed conflict, hostilities, civil war, insurrection, or an exceptional fact of nature.[214]

160. Another circumstance of strict liability with constitutional origin is the strict liability of the state, established in Article 37, paragraph 6: "legal persons of public or private law that perform public services will be responsible for the harm caused by their agents … to third parties." In addition to the constitutional norm of Article 37, 6, the Civil Code of 2002 regulates the strict liability of the state in its Article 43, where "the legal persons of internal public law are liable civilly by their acts and their agents for any harm caused to third parties."[215]

161. The Civil Code of 2002 establishes strict liability, along with other legal statutes that regulate specific cases. Regarding services and products,[216] it states that the strict liability of the transporter for harms caused to people and luggage transported is established in Article 734; in addition, the strict liability of the entrepreneur for products in circulation is given by Article 931.

162. Regarding indirect liability for the actions of others or vicarious liability,[217] the Civil Code of 2002 established that these are: the strict liability of parents for harm caused by acts performed by their underage children, and the caretaker and tutor's liability for acts performed by their pupils in Article 932, I, combined with Article 933; the firm owner's liability or commitment for the acts of employees, servants and agents in Article 932, III, combined with Article 933; the strict liability of the owners of hotels, bed and breakfasts, houses or establishments where one can find shelter for money for acts performed by their guests, tenants and students in Article 932, IV combined with Article 933; and the strict liability of persons who have freely participated in the product of crimes in proportion to their participation for the harm done by criminals in Article 932, V, combined with Article 933. The rule of the strict liability of parents, tutors and caretakers is given by Article 928,

---

214. The application of the excluding factors established by Arts 6 and 8 of law 6.453 of 1977 after the Federal Constitution of 1988, with the adoption of the integral risk theory is a controversial matter. *See* PAULA, *As excludentes de Responsabilidade Civil Objetiva,* 2007, São Paulo, at 83–86, and, STJ, 2ª Turma, REsp. 1180888/GO, Relator Ministro Herman Benjamin, DJe 28.02.2012. Brasília.
215. *See* Part I, Ch. 1, §2. Liability of Public Authorities (Governmental Liability).
216. *See* Part III, Ch. 2. Product Liability and Ch. 3. Liability for Service.
217. *See* Part II, Ch. 1. Vicarious Liability and Ch. 2. Liability of Parents, Teachers and Instructors (For Children, Minors, and Students).

caput and text, which states the subsidiary and mitigated liability of anyone without the capacity to practice the acts of civil life (persons under the age of 16, persons who are ill, and persons with mental illnesses) with regard to persons who care for them: "the incapable person is responsible for the harm he/she may cause, if the people who are responsible for him/her are not obliged to be so or do not have the resources to pay the damages," and the damages "will not be payable if they deprive the incapable person or people that depend on him of the resources necessary for existence."

163. As for the indirect liability for an act or thing or animal or liability for things and animals,[218] the Civil Code establishes strict liability for accidents caused by animals, set out in Article 936; strict liability for ruin and construction in Article 937; and strict liability for harm caused by things falling or thrown from buildings in Article 938.

164. In addition to establishing strict liability in the normative statutes that regulate the specific cases mentioned, the Civil Code also establishes strict liability through general clauses with an open content. The abuse of rights,[219] qualified in Article 187 as the exercise of a right with manifest excess in the light of the "limits imposed by its economic or social goals as well as good faith and good custom," leads to the strict liability of the owner of the rights for the harms caused by the abusive act or omission.

165. One of the main innovations made by the Civil Code of 2002 is the general clause of strict liability for the activity risk provided by Article 927: "there will be an obligation to repair the harm caused, independently of fault, in cases specified in law, or when the activity regularly carried out by the author of the harm author implies, by its nature, risks to the rights of others."[220] Along with the general clause of strict liability for dangerous activities of Article 927, this has significantly expanded the courts' possibilities of acting. They are explicitly authorized to qualify some activities as dangerous, thus making them subject to the application of strict liability. Thus, it is possible to say that Brazil has changed from a closed civil law system, as in the case of Germany, to a mixed civil law system, similar to that in Italy and Portugal, making significant progress in promoting the harmonious action of the legislature and the judiciary in the process of defining what activities are subject to strict liability.[221] The statement of Schreiber is enlightening:[222]

---

218. *See* Part II, Ch. 3. Liability for Things and Animals.
219. *See* Part I, Ch. 2, §3. Abuse of Rights.
220. In this particular, the Brazilian system of torts is in line with institutes such as the principles of European tort law (Art. 5:101. abnormally dangerous activities), elaborated by the European Group on Tort Law, and the Restatement of the Law Third, Torts: Liability for Physical and Emotional Harm (§20. Abnormally Dangerous Activities), made by The American Law Institute. *See* BATTESINI, Comparison of Tort Law Systems from the Perspective of Economic Efficiency: Brazilian Civil Code, Principles of European Law and Restatements of the Law, New York, SSRN, 2015, at 7–8, http://ssrn.com/abstract=2595790.
221. *See* BATTESINI, Comparative Tort Law and Economics: Strict Liability in Brazilian Legal Practice, New York, SSRN, 2013, at 26, http://ssrn.com/abstract=2263506.

the general clause of strict liability directs itself to hazardous activities, which is to say to activities that presents a high level of risk, either because they involve intrinsically harmful goods (as radioactive, explosive and weaponry materials, etc.), or because they use methods with a high potential for harm (such as the control of hydrological resources, nuclear energy manipulation, etc.). The definition, although elastic, of a list of activities covered in the application scope of the sole paragraph of Article 927, is a task appointed to jurisprudential action and to doctrinal investigations.

166. With an open clause, the core of the problem that presents itself to the judiciary is in the characterization of dangerous activities. In this context, the establishment of clear and objective directives acquires relevance, through the consideration of factors such as the probability of elevated accident rates, the magnitude of expected damages and the impossibility of avoidance of accidents, even through the adoption of adequate precautions.[223] In applying the general clause of Article 927 of the Civil Code, the jurisprudence has qualified as dangerous activities the generation and distribution of electric energy,[224] the construction of dams[225] and transportation of items of monetary value.[226]

---

222. *See* SCHREIBER, *Novos Paradigmas da Responsabilidade Civil, da Erosão dos Filtros da Reparação à Diluição dos Danos*, 2009, São Paulo, at 25.
223. *See* BATTESINI, *Direito e Economia, Novos Horizontes no Estudo da Responsabilidade Civil no Brasil*, 2011, São Paulo, at 240–241.
224. *See* STJ, 4ª Turma, REsp 896.568/CE, Relator Ministro Luis Felipe Salomão, DJ. 30.06.2009, p. 233. Brasília.
225. *See* STJ, 4ª Turma, REsp 1374342/MG, Relator Ministro Luis Felipe Salomão, DJe. 25.09.2013. Brasília.
226. *See* STJ, 3ª Turma, REsp 185659/SP, Relator Ministro Carlos Alberto Menezes Direito, DJ 18.09.2000 p. 126. Brasília.

Part IV. Defenses and Exception Clauses

Chapter 1. Limitation of Action (Suspension and Interruption)

167. Brazilian law adopts, as a rule, the "whole reparation principle," which means ideally "putting the injured party into an equivalent situation to that before the act."[227] This principle can be perceived "in its most broad dimension … when pecuniary damage is considered;"[228] thus losses must be estimated to compensate the harmed party as a whole. This principle is set out in the caput of Article 944 of the Civil Code ("The damages are measured by the extent of the harm"), but it has its limitations.

168. The first of them can be extracted by the paragraph of the same Article 944, since it is established there that "if there is an excessive disproportion between the degree of fault and the damage, the judge can reduce the damage proportionally." This is about balancing the whole reparation principle with the proportionality postulate, which derives, in turn, from the notion of a broad sense of equity, and which, exceptionally, attributes importance and intensity to the responsible fault, and also allows, "in some measure, a return to a prior stage of great, light and least fault."[229]

169. As Sanseverino states:[230]

> the main clause of damage reduction, set out in the normative clause of the Article 944 text of the CC/2002, gives to the judge the power/duty to proceed to an equitable solution to a specific scenario, in cases of excessive disproportion between the degree of fault of the agent and the severity of the harms suffered by the victim. In deciding the amount of the damages, three distinctive elements are taken into consideration, relevant in legal fact-related situations: (a) the degree of fault; (b) the extent of the harm; (c) any excessive disproportion between the fault and the damage.

As highlighted by the same author:

---

227. *See* SANSEVERINO, *Princípio da Reparação Integral*, 2013, São Paulo, at 19.
228. *Ibid.*, at 49.
229. *See* DIREITO & CAVALIERI FILHO, *Comentários ao Novo Código Civil*, 2007, Rio de Janeiro, at 338.
230. *See* SANSEVERINO, *Princípio da Reparação Integral*, 2013, São Paulo, at 99.

the first element to be considered in terms of the application of the general clause of damage reduction is the fault of the agent. Unlike what happens with Article 186 of the Civil Code, in which the intent and fault are considered the same for the configuration of the illicit purposes, the expression "fault" from the text of Article 944 must be taken in its strict sense (culpa *stricto sensu*), not having the incidence of reduction regarding the intended acts.

As for the second aspect, "the harm suffered by the victim must be severe, considering not only its objective extent, but also the economic value of the corresponding damages ... " and "the nature of the harm suffered by the victim must also be considered; thus, if the harmed interests are only patrimonial, related to material harms provoked by the illicit behavior (e.g., traffic accident caused by a slight fault with extensive damage, though only material), the norm in question can be considered fully applicable ... "[231] Finally, concerning the necessity of avoiding disproportion, Sanseverino[232] states that:

> the expression "excessive disproportion" means that the disequilibrium between the degree of fault and the extent of the harm must be logical, and must be observed through the formulation of a reasonable judgment, which is the criterion to be used by the judge in making a reduction.

170. Another limitation may be found in the rule laid down in the text of Article 928 of the Civil Code. In the caput is set out the civil liability of those incapable, and equity is invoked ("The damages set out in this article must be equitable, and will not apply if they deprive of the necessary means incapable persons or dependent persons"). The fact that the "integral reparation principle" indicates not only the so-called "compensatory function" (or "reparation") of tort law, but also what Sanseverino[233] has called an "indemnifying function" deserves quoting: "the extent of the harm constitutes the maximum limit for damages." This aspect (limitation) of the content of Article 944 of the Civil Code leads a great proportion of Brazilian doctrine[234] to consider punitive damages incompatible with the Brazilian system. Though the matter is not considered settled (there are positions in the contrary sense),[235] the reality is that "punitive damages" are admitted in practice by the Brazilian courts, by the establishment of non-pecuniary damages (or "moral damages"), without defined criteria (each case is considered on its merits), under the

---

231. *Ibid.*, at 107.
232. *Ibid.*, at 107.
233. *See* SANSEVERINO, *Princípio da Reparação Integral*, 2013, São Paulo, at 59.
234. *See* MIRANDA, *Tratado de direito privado*, 2003, Campinas; SILVA, *O dano moral e sua reparação*, 1969, Rio de Janeiro; GONÇALVES, *Direito civil brasileiro. Responsabilidade civil*, 2010, São Paulo; THEODORO JUNIOR, *Comentários ao novo código civil*, 2003, Rio de Janeiro; MORAES, *Danos à pessoa humana: uma leitura civil-constitucional dos danos extrapatrimoniais* 2003, São Paulo; and, SANSEVERINO, *Princípio da Reparação Integral*, 2010, São Paulo.
235. *See* PEREIRA, *Responsabilidade Civil*, 2012, Rio de Janeiro; DINIZ, *Curso de direito civil brasileiro*. São Paulo, 2009; BITTAR, *Responsabilidade civil: teoria e prática*, 1990, Rio de Janeiro; CAVALIERI FILHO, *Programa de responsabilidade civil*, 2010, São Paulo; FIUZA, *Direito civil. Curso completo*, 2010, Belo Horizonte; ANDRADE, *Dano moral e indenização punitiva: os*

argument of the "pedagogic function" of civil liability (in contrast with the deterrent and punitive functions of tort law).[236]

171.   Other limitations on the full application of the generic norms of civil liability may be identified in cases of special immunity, spinning off from constitutional statements or special laws. There is the case of parliamentary immunity (caput of Article 53 of the Federal Constitution), where members of parliament cannot be held as defendants in civil (or criminal) law for their opinions, words and votes, the Supreme Court (*Supremo Tribunal Federal*)[237] restricting this limitation to the typical exercise of the activity of legislating. Another case of immunity applies to attorneys, to their acts and statements in the exercise of their profession (Law no. 8,906/ 94, Article 2, §1, and Article 7, §2), with the restrictions stated in the same legal document (The Attorney's Statute/*Estatuto da Advocacia*). It is not rare, though, for immunity cases to be dismissed in situations of abuse of rights.[238] It is worth highlighting that, in Brazilian law, diplomatic immunities do not reach the realm of civil liability.

---

punitive damages na experiência do common law e na perspectiva do direito brasileiro, 2009, Rio de Janeiro; and, VENTURI, *Responsabilidade Civil Preventiva*, 2014, São Paulo.
236. *See* SANTOLIM, *Nexo de Causalidade e Prevenção na Responsabilidade Civil no Direito Brasileiro e Português*. RIDB, Ano 3 (2014), nº 10, available at http://www.idb-fdul.com.
237. *See* STJ, HC nº 81.730, Relator o Ministro NELSON JOBIM, julgado em 01/08/2003. Brasília.
238. *See* Ch. 1, §4.

Chapter 2. Grounds of Justification

172. For the exclusion of civil liability exemption clauses (necessity state, regular exercise of rights and self-defense) and cases of causation exemption (exclusive victim's accident, concurrent causation, third-party accident, chance, and act of God) must be taken into consideration. The statutory limitations still deserve attention; these are not specific to tort law, but also belong to the realm of efficacy.

§1. Consent

173. There are no specific provisions in the Brazilian Civil Code about "non-solicitation clauses,"[239] which are "the stipulation by one of the hiring parties, with the permission of the other, that it will not be liable for events of harm experienced by the other, resulting from the non-execution or inadequate execution of a contract, which without the clause would be compensated to the party."[240] This situation is restricted to contractual liability, which is outside the object of this study. However, it is worth referring to the great debate present in Brazilian doctrine[241] and jurisprudence[242] about the validity of this clause. Cases in which there could be a "tacit consent" of the injured party occur when, in consideration of his/her behavior, the harmed party contributes to the occurrence of the accident; these cases will be studied in the light of cases of "victim accidents."

§2. Exemption Clauses

174. According to Article 188 of the Civil Code, "do not constitute illicit acts: I – those carried out in self-defense or in the regular exercise of a recognized right; II – damage to or destruction of other's belongings, or harm to a person to remove imminent danger." In addition, the text of the same article states that, "in the case of II, the act will be legal only while the circumstances are absolutely necessary, not exceeding the limits indispensable for the removal of the danger." The illicit exclusion, as a rule, excludes civil liability, but, as seen above (Part I, Chapter 1, §1), there may be civil liability even without illicit acts. This is what can be understood by the disposition of Article 929 of the Civil Code, where it states "if the harmed person, or the thing's owner, in the case of II of Article 188, is not to blame

---

239. Which motivates the critiques of RODRIGUES, Direito Civil – vol. 4 – Responsabilidade Civil, 2002, São Paulo, at 182.
240. *See* RODRIGUES, *supra* at 239.
241. *See* DIAS, *Cláusula de não-indenizar*, 1980, Rio de Janeiro.
242. There is no great controversy about the theme of the consumer relations, when the consumer is a natural person (the clause is considered invalid, due the disposition of the Art. 51, I, da Lei n° 8.078/90 – CDC). As for transportation contracts, the theme was the subject of the *Sumula* 161 of the Supreme Federal Court ("In transportation contracts, the non-solicitation clause is invalid"). As for contracts in which there are no consumer relations, the jurisprudence has adopted contradictory positions (while against in Civil Appeal, *Apelação Cível* n° 2000000403415-1/000, of TJMG, *Apelação Cível* n° 9145437-46.2005.8.26.0000, do TJSP is favorable, as shown in the Civil Appeal).

for the danger, damages for the harm suffered are due." This means that even if the act is licit (thus there was a pre-exclusion of the illicit nature), civil liability will arise. The rule of Article 930 adds that "in the case of II of Article 188, if the danger arises by the fault of a third party, the author of the harm has the right of redress to compensate the damages paid to the injured party." Finally, in the text of the same article: "the same action will compete against one who in self-defense has caused the harm (Article 188, I)." In other words, the harmful act will be licit, but the agent must pay damages to the injured party (civil liability), with the right of redress against the person who created the danger or act of aggression which originated the need for self-defense.

I. Necessity State

175. The necessity state is an exemption clause related to Article 171, which limits the application ambit of civil liability in extreme cases where a person, in order to prevent a great danger or harm to himself or third parties, inflicts harm on another. According to Theodoro Junior:[243]

> The necessity state occurs when a person involves himself in a factual situation, in which, to remove an imminent danger, he is compelled to sacrifice another person or another person's property. In the realm of interests, though the agent's conduct is licit, it will in some cases be in conflict with the worthy interests of the person who suffered the harm necessary to save the rights of the first person. Even though the law states the licit act (lack of illicit), in Article 188, II, the agent will not be always free from the obligation to compensate the harm to the person who suffered the consequences of the rescue act of the person or thing under risk. Therefore, if the victim is the person who gave rise to the danger, he/she will not be able to complain about the harm suffered to remove the risk created. But, if the injured person (owner of the harmed goods) did not contribute to the origin of the dangerous situation, the Code imposes on the agent the obligation to pay damages for the harm, even though he/she acted to exercise a right recognized by the legal order (Article 929). It is not, though, through the illicit nature of the act that such liability will be imposed, but on the basis of the fact-act that the law values as a good resolving a conflict of interest. The duty to pay damages, in the Code's system does not emerge only from the illicit (Article 927). Many other causes also generate the same liability, among them, fact acts and even simple licit facts.

176. The author also reminds us that for "a legitimate reaction, authorized by Article 188, to take place, it is demanded that the agent be put in an unavoidable situation of having to preserve his own property through the sacrifice of another's."[244]

---

243. *See* THEODORO JUNIOR, *Comentários ao Novo Código Civil*, 2003, Rio de Janeiro, at 141.
244. *Ibid.*, at 143.

II. Due Use of Rights

177. As the "abuse of rights" defines an objective illicit hypothesis, as demonstrated (Part I, Chapter 2, §3), the "due" use of a recognized right does not allow any other solution than the legality of the act, even though it may cause harm. As the doctrine recalls, acts practiced by a creditor in the enforced execution of the obligation (*ex vi*, protest, attachment, arrestment, bid) are harmful to the debtor, but they do not create the right to civil compensation, and thus are licit acts. The necessity required is that the due exercise of rights is carried out in a "regular" manner in order to demarcate it from a situation of abuse. As Theodoro Junior recalls:[245]

> Ethical values being at stake, it is hard for the legislator to translate them, hypothetically, into positive norms. It will always fall under the prudent criteria of the judge, regarding the circumstances of the specific case, to identify where the due use of a right is indicated and where its exercise becomes abusive. It is in this field that reasonable logic is required, not pure logic.
>
> As Pereira comments, the individual, in acting within his right, "must confine himself to the realm of reasonableness." If this limit is trespassed, by a person who exercises faculties that are technically his right, and provokes an unnecessary or unjust evil, that agent "will incur a compensatory duty."
>
> The exercise of a person's own right cannot violate the rights of another. The rights of every person end where the rights of others begin. In every conflict of rights – which have only a shade of conflict – the legal order and its general criteria are used to define whose interests must prevail and whose interests are meant to be passed over. Therefore, the abusive exercise of a right occurs, precisely when the right's owner prevails himself of it to harm a third party who has the right to oppose to him, to avoid the harm the first wants to inflict on him.
>
> "In truth, there is no right against right; and it is absurd that the exercise of one's own right could lead to the violation of another's right, as the law cannot protect at the same time the interests of the harmed and the agent of the harm."
>
> "Which is why, by exercising in an irregular manner his right to cause harm to another, who legally does not have the obligation to tolerate this, the right's owner exits the licit realm and enters the illicit one (Article 187)."

III. Self-Defense

178. There is no concept of "self-defense" in the Civil Code, for the reason that the doctrine employs a definition presented in Article 25 of the Brazilian Criminal Code ("it can be understood as in self-defense when a person using the necessary moderate means counters unjust aggression, current or imminent to his/her or

---

245. *Ibid.*

another's right"). Noronha invoked Dias to say that "self-defense is a qualified necessity state."[246] As Theodoro Junior affirms:[247]

> the Civil Code states that "acts practiced in self-defense do not constitute illicit acts" (Art. 188, I). The civil rules do not configure this through the description of its elements or requisites. Therefore, it is in the criminal law that the private applier will find the means to conceptualize the illicit exemption clause ... First, it is extracted from the criminal concept that the victim of self-defense can be used to dispel the aggression to his/her own as for other goods. In addition, the following prerequisites cataloged by the Criminal Code (Art. 21) need to be demonstrated so that the agent can benefit from the exemption clause of self-defense: (a) current or imminent and unjust aggression; (b) the preservation of a right of his/her own or of another; (c) use of moderate means necessary to defense. Preemptive aggression against future harms that are remotely predictable is not considered as self-defense. It is necessary that the reaction is against a current or imminent evil, that the attacked person was not able to defend himself in any other fashion than by the immediate use of force to preserve himself or his property. A person must act, though, in the fashion strictly necessary to dispel the threatening harm that threatens him/her. The degree of aggression should not become retaliation or vendetta. The excessive use of force for defense is off-limits to the licit field and constitutes an abuse of rights, turning it into illicit act beyond what is necessary to dispel the unjust aggression (Art. 187).

§3. EXEMPTION FROM CAUSATION

179. On some occasions, someone who is liable for a harmful fact can demonstrate that the harm is not effectively connected to him/her by the act practiced (partially or entirely), and actually arises for another reason, connected to the other agent, and therefore interrupting the causation nexus. This replaces the incidence of a determined cause with the determination of the existence of another, usually more relevant, from which originates the exclusion of civil liability of one of the authors.[248]

I. Victim's Exclusive Fact

180. The victim's exclusive fault occurs when the acts of the agents are not relevant to the configuration of the harm itself, but the victim's own acts are. In the definition of Noronha,[249] "as the expression indicates, the incident of harm ... is

---

246. *See* NORONHA, *Direito das Obrigações*, 2010, São Paulo, at 375.
247. *See* THEODORO JUNIOR, *Comentários ao Novo Código Civil*, 2003, Rio de Janeiro, at 137.
248. *See* CRUZ, *O Problema do Nexo Causal na Responsabilidade* Civil, 2005, Rio de Janeiro, at 155.
249. *See* NORONHA, *Direito das Obrigações*, 2010, São Paulo, at 620.

attributed to the act of the person who suffered the harm. When the actuation of the harm arises from him or herself, there is no reason to discuss paying damages (except on special occasions of great strict liability)." The victim's act, in this case, is not limited to contributing to the harm (a situation that will be analyzed below), but is the exclusive cause of the harmful act, making its imputation to another agent unjustified.

II. Third-Party Act

181. According to the same reasoning, third-party acts are those connected to the acts of another, as opposed to the main agent, being liable for the harm, as Noronha states: "the third party act is a causation excluding (and therefore, usually also an exemption clause) an anti-juridical act carried out by someone who is not the injured party … The third party's act cannot exclude liability in great strict liability cases. On the other hand, it may be the very determinant of the other's liability, when the harm is caused by a person, independently of the one who was first *identified* as the agent; in these cases, it can be considered as liability for the act of *an* other."

III. Chance and Act of God

182. Chance and the acts of God are situations where no single human being can resist, being connected to natural or collective human phenomena. As states Noronha states:[250]

> When the expressions Chance *or* Act of God are used in the strict sense (and without distinguishing chance from an act of God) they encompass natural facts such as storms, floods and diseases (which can be named acts of God), and human actions, not individualized, such as war, robbery, depredations, and even demonstrations of authority, always where the facts determine the harm caused. The imposition of an authority that has generated a harm, is traditionally called factum principis. Human actions that are not individualized which, together with natural facts are related to chance and acts of God in the strict sense, are often close to third party acts. Therefore, for instance, if a third party's act is the reason for the loss of goods transported by a truck, as a result of a collision with another truck, when the other truck is out of control, the loss could be considered as due to chance or an act of God; also when the goods were stolen in an assault with guns led by a gang.

---

250. *See Ibid.*, at 621.

IV. Contributory Causation

183. The situation of co-causality identifies the participation of different agents which may result in joint liability (in the case of co-authors, as the text of Article 942 of the Civil Code states), or liability mitigation (the case described in Article 945 of the same Code). Even though the reference is to "fault" in Article 945, it is actually about the causation contribution of the injured party to the occurrence of the harm itself, as Cruz states,[251] through the connection to Dias. As Lisboa observes,[252] the participation of the injured party in the occurrence (or in the dimension) of the harm having been established, from three possible solutions ("the proportional division of suffered losses," "the proportionality of fault of each co-authors" and "the degree of participation of each in the causation of the result"), "the causation principle must prevail for the purpose of determining compensation for the harm." The system adopted by Brazilian law is very close to the comparative negligence of common law.[253] It is not precisely about "lack of causation" (and, therefore, the "exclusion of civil liability") but, more precisely, about acknowledging the presence of another cause, with the mitigation of the responsible agent (through the application of the proportionality rule), due to the conclusion that the harm only acquired its total dimension from the joint collaboration of agent and victim.

§4. STATUTORY LIMITATIONS

184. According to Article 206, §3, V, of the Brazilian Civil Code, a "claim for civil compensation" is limited to three years. In consumer relations, in the terms of Article 27 of Law no. 8,078/90 (CDC), "compensation for harms caused by products or services is limited to five years." The statutory limitations, in any case, despite their not extinguishing the right to compensation (if the agent of the harm complies this will be the due fulfillment of the obligation), will prevent the possibility of the injured party demanding reparation via judicial and extrajudicial procedures.

---

251. *See* CRUZ, *O Problema do Nexo Causal na Responsabilidade Civil*, 2005, Rio de Janeiro, at 343.
252. *See* LISBOA, *Manual de Direito Civil*, vol. 2 – *Obrigações e Responsabilidade Civil*, 2004, São Paulo, at 521.
253. Contrary to what the expression "contributory causation" or "contributory fault" may suggest, in common law concurrent negligence is more adequate to the situation of complementary causation discussed in Part IV.

Part V. Causation

185. There is not, in Brazilian law, a specific rule about causation in the tort system. However, doctrine[254] and jurisprudence[255] recognize in Article 403 of the Civil Code (which gives the rules for loss and harm) the basis for the recognition of the criteria for causation. In this article, it is written that "even if the non-execution results from the debtor's intent, the loss and harms will include only the effective harms and loss of profit from its immediate and direct effect." Even though it seems evident that this rule is directed to contractual liability, (the expression "non-execution" indicates this), the lack of any other indication of that theme in positive law anchors the theme to this article.

186. As is known, the first theories about causation emerging in continental law are derivations of philosophical conceptions about the subject and, in that sense, had as their starting point the idea of "physics" or "mechanics," or even "natural" causation. As Hart and Honoré state,[256] the expression is a modern version of the notion *versari in re illicita* as discussed by Glaser (1858), in Austria, and immediately afterward by von Buri, in Germany (1860), with the idea that any necessary condition or *sine qua non* of an event is its causation. This was the emergence of the *Bedingungstheorie*, or condition theory or equivalence of condition theory. According to this starting point, it is possible to see adequate causation as an essay of sophistication, in order to specify the notion of cause. The same can be affirmed of variants of adequate causation, such as direct (and immediate) harm.

187. In another strand of thought is positioned norm protection theory, which identifies the notion of cause in the normative element (axiological), depriving it of any naturalistic link and approximating it to the attribution factor. As has been stated, condition equivalency theory does not distinguish causation and condition: if any conditions act together to produce the same result, all of them have the same value (all of them are equal). Therefore, in order to know whether a determined condition is the cause, it will be mentally excluded in a hypothetical process: if the same result no longer follows, the condition in question constitutes the causation. In the evolution of this theory is found adequate causality, which individualizes or qualifies the condition. Cause is the antecedent that is not only necessary, but also sufficient for the production of the result. Therefore, not every condition is a cause of

---

254. *See* CRUZ, *O Problema do Nexo Causal na Responsabilidade Civil*, 2005, Rio de Janeiro, at 97.
255. STJ, REsp 1557978/DF, 03/11/15. Brasilia.
256. *See* HART and HONORÉ, *Causation in the Law*, 1959, Oxford, at 442–443.

the fact, only those conditions that are more appropriate to produce the event. Following the same authors (p. 466), von Bar was the precursor (1870) of what is called the "generalization school," taking as a starting point the work of Glaser, though contesting his conclusion that any condition must be considered as a cause. For von Bar, any cause is necessarily a condition, but not any condition is a cause; thus a causal quality can only be given to these events that are outside "regularity" ("regular" or "ordinary," events, therefore, even if they are conditions, are not causes). This theory was later developed by von Kries (1880), who incorporated elements of probabilistic analysis into the notion of "regularity of events" proposed by von Bar.[257] According to Noronha,[258] the theory admits a "positive" formulation ("a fact must be considered an adequate cause of a posterior event when it favors its production") and "negative" ("the cause is adequate that, following the rules of experience, is not irrelevant to the emergence of the harm"), considering as preferable the second. It is sustained as applicable in the Brazilian Law ordainment.[259]

188. A variant of the last theory is the "direct harm" affirmed in Brazil by Alvim; thus "the cause of a harm can be a close or remote fact, but it must be directly connected to it." In the Supreme Federal Court (*Supremo Tribunal Federal*), on the occasion of the RE 130764/PR trial, the Rapporteur, Minister Moreira Alves, affirmed that this theory is the basis for causation in Brazilian civil law. This is also the position of, among others, Gonçalves.[260] Cruz[261] details the Brazilian doctrine's perspective about this theory.[262] Other variants of adequate causation are "efficient causation" and "preponderant causation."[263] In the direction of a rupture with the "naturalistic" idea of cause, is the idea that states that is not possible to identify a sole criterion to define the causation in every hypothesis of civil liability.[264] Finally, and from a strictly normative perspective, are the theories that state the strict imputation of causation (encompassing, therefore, the attribution factor and the causation nexus), which have no particular influence in Brazil.[265]

189. It is worth mentioning, in the causation doctrine in civil liability, the idea of multiple causes, which can be presented in many forms. As a rule, the condition *sine qua non*, criterion or necessary condition, is accepted in private law doctrine as the minimum necessary for the causation, which would give the maximum notion of causation, though this procedure could lead to strange results in cases of multiple

---

257. *See* SANTOLIM, *Nexo de Causalidade e Prevenção na Responsabilidade Civil*, Revista da AJURIS – v. 41 – n. 136 – December 2014, Porto Alegre.
258. *See* NORONHA, *Direito das Obrigações*, 2010, São Paulo, at 601–602.
259. *Ibid.*, at 603.
260. *See* GONÇALVES, Direito Civil Brasileiro, 2007, São Paulo, at 333–334.
261. *See* CRUZ, *O Problema do Nexo Causal na Responsabilidade Civil*, 2005, Rio de Janeiro, at 107.
262. In addition, the courts remain using the "adequate causation theory," as in REsp 1698726/RJ, Jun. 1, 2021.
263. For a deeper comprehension of the theories, *see* CRUZ, *supra*, 2005.
264. *See* SANTOLIM, *Nexo de Causalidade e Prevenção na Responsabilidade Civil*, Revista da AJURIS – v. 41 – n. 136 – December 2014, Porto Alegre.
265. *See* CRUZ, *O Problema do Nexo Causal na Responsabilidade Civil*, 2005, Rio de Janeiro, at 122.

causes. Under a hypothesis of cumulative causation, the result could be equally produced without any one single cause, and thus no single cause is a necessary condition.

190. Another problem considered as relevant to the subject is "virtual" or "hypothetical" causation (a fact given as adequate to the production of the result, though not sufficient to produce it, due to another fact that alters the causation chain), which generates what Noronha[266] details as interrupted causation (when the real *causa* is invoked by the author of the virtual cause – this is the positive relevance of the virtual cause) or anticipated causation (when the author of the real cause is the one who alleges the existence of a virtual cause – which constitutes the negative relevance of the virtual cause). In a general sense, legal relevance is denied to "virtual causes," even though they exist, as the author affirms, in "more complex situations," from which can be highlighted the mitigation of the value of damages.

191. "Complementary causation," which occurs when "two actions would only cause the harm together, the complementarity of the causes being necessary (e.g., two doses of poison, which by themselves are not lethal, dispensed into coffee by two different persons together causing a person's death),"[267] is worthy of consideration in Brazilian law.[268] The causes can be presented in simultaneous or successive ways, in any case there being no problem of "super-determination of causation" in the light of the dispositions of the text of Article 942 of the Brazilian Civil Code ("the authors with the co-authors are liable in solidarity").

192. Though not necessarily forming cumulative causation,[269] "each action was by itself a cause, which is enough to cause the harmful event (for instance, two mortal doses of poison dropped into the same coffee by two different persons)."[270] In this context, the distinction mentioned by Acciarri,[271] between conditions NESS (necessary element of a sufficient set) and INUS (insufficient but non-redundant part of an unnecessary but sufficient condition) gains importance. By adopting the first criterion, as mentioned by Hart and Honoré,[272] in cases of super-determination of causation, each necessary element of these bundles is "eligible" as a cause.

---

266. *See* NORONHA, *Direito das Obrigações*, 2010, São Paulo, at 658.
267. *See* PINTO, *Sobre Condição e Causa na Responsabilidade Civil*, 2008, Coimbra, at 933.
268. *See* LISBOA, *Manual de Direito Civil*, vol. 2 – *Obrigações e Responsabilidade Civil*, 2004, São Paulo, at 518.
269. The expression was coined by PINTO, at 933.
270. *See* ACCIARRI, *La Relación de Causalidad y las Funciones del Derecho de Daños*, 2009, Buenos Aires, at 22. According to the author, the terms were coined by J.L. Mackie.
271. *Supra* at 112.
272. Critiques of the use of NESS and their refutations can be found in WRIGHT, The NESS Account of Natural Causation: A Response to Criticisms. Available at http://scholarship.kentlaw.iit.edu/fac_schol/716. Published: Jan. 1, 2011. Accessed on May 12, 2014. In this work, Wright distinguishes the NESS criteria of the two others attributed to Hart and Honoré ("factor with causality relevance") and John Mackie (conditions INUS).

193. The Brazilian doctrine[273] recognizes, in addition, alternative causation in which is "uncertainty about which, of a variety of causes, was the one that produced the result."[274] Alternatively, in the description of Noronha,[275] this is a situation where "there are two or more facts with the potential to cause a determined harm, but it is not known which one is the true cause."

---

273. *See* LISBOA, Manual de Direito Civil, vol. 2 – Obrigações e Responsabilidade Civil, 2004, São Paulo, at 518.
274. *See* PINTO, *Sobre Condição e Causa na Responsabilidade Civil*, 2008, Coimbra, at 933.
275. *See* NORONHA, *Direito das Obrigações*, 2010, São Paulo, at 652.

Part VI. Remedies

Chapter 1. General Principles

194. Harm is an element or essential requisite, a condition *sine qua non* for civil liability. It results in the torts system in the obligation to pay damages, and therefore, logically it cannot be fulfilled where there is nothing to repair. The notion of harm supposes that the victim has been harmed by a situation not of his/her fruition, being deprived of a former advantage. Therefore, in the legal realm, in essence, the notion of harm is related to the damage caused to the victim, the subtraction of a value or good.[276] In the formal definition of Cavalieri Filho: "harm is the subtraction or diminution of a legal good, whatever its nature, being either a patrimonial good, or a part of the person of the victim, such as his honor, image, liberty, etc ... ."[277]

195. The economic notion of damage is analogous to the legal notion. As Cooter and Ulen register, "Harm has a simple economic interpretation: a downward shift in the victim's utility or profit function," the goal of damages being the restitution of the integrity of the victim.[278] It can be inferred, then, from the legal or economic perspective, that the basic idea inherent in the harm element is connected to the damage, to the reparation or compensation, so that the victim can return to the situation he was in before the harm or can be compensated for the modification of his/her status. In other words, the basic idea inherent in the element of harm is tied to the victim's damages to correct the external defects caused by the acts carried out by the author – the negative externalities.[279]

196. The reparation of harms, the correction of the external effects of the act practiced by the author, can be specific, such as the reconstruction of the situation of a situation prior to the harm, or can be equivalent, through the delivery of pecuniary values to the victim. Though the obligation to pay damages can be fulfilled through the restoration of the debtor's property to the condition prior to the harmful event (natural reparation or *in natura*), it is more usual for damages to take the form

---

276. *See* DIAS, *Da Responsabilidade Civil*, Rio de Janeiro, 2006, at 969, and PEREIRA, *Responsabilidade Civil*, 2012. Rio de Janeiro, at 54–56.
277. *See* CAVALIERI FILHO, *Programa de Responsabilidade Civil*, 2012, São Paulo, at 73.
278. *See* COOTER & ULEN, *Law and Economics*, 2008, Boston, at 326 and 389.
279. *See* BATTESINI, *Direito e Economia, Novos Horizontes no Estudo da Responsabilidade Civil no Brasil*, 2011, São Paulo, at 250.

of a pecuniary nature, to be fulfilled by the delivery to the creditor of money corresponding to compensation for the patrimonial or extra-patrimonial losses suffered.[280] In practice, the attribution of responsibility for harm assumes that it can be evaluated and calculated, which, in its turn, assumes that it is possible to isolate the harm and attribute a monetary value to it or to restore the victim to the prior status quo. In cases where it is not possible to determine a monetary amount which allows the victim to be indifferent between a world with the losses and a world without the losses (such as, for example, severe injuries, death, etc.), the solution is to determine a monetary value which can at least bring some additional utility to the victim's dependents.[281]

197. The association of the compensation idea, the reestablishment or restoration of a prior situation, that would exist if the harmful event had not happened, with the pecuniary character of damages, has its corollary in the classic legal rule of monetary correspondence between damages and the harm, and the proportionality or symmetry between them. This symmetry is crystallized in the civil liability doctrine, and can be found in the Brazilian system in the caput of Article 944 of the Brazilian Civil Code of 2002, which expressly establishes that "damages are measured by the extent of the harm."[282]

198. In the Brazilian Civil Code of 2002, civil liability (Title IX) is regulated in two chapters. In Chapter 1, the Code establishes the necessary elements to characterize the duty to pay damages, encompassing a general clause of reparation for harm in Article 927: "a person who, by an illicit act, causes harm to other, is obliged to repair it." In Chapter 2, the Code treats the theme of damages, establishing the general principles of liquidation of harm in Articles 944–947. In addition, in the same articles, the Code regulates the specific aspects related to damages in specific cases such as homicide (Articles 948 and 951); injuries or offenses to health (Articles 949, 950 and 951); usurpation or divestment of another's property (Article 952); injury, defamation, or calumny (Article 953); and offenses to personal liberty (Article 954). It must be highlighted, in addition, that the Brazilian judiciary has developed an important role in the definition of the reparable harms and the establishing the criteria for the obligation to pay damages.

---

280. *See* ANDRADE, *Dano Moral e Indenização Punitiva: Os Punitive Damages na Experiência da Common Law e na Perspectiva do Direito Brasileiro*, 2009, Rio de Janeiro, at 141, and COELHO, *Curso de Direito Civil, Responsabilidade Civil*, 2005, São Paulo, at 397–398.
281. *See* SCHAEFFER, HAND-BERND AND KLAUS, OTT, *Economic Analysis of Civil Law*, 2004, Cheltenham, at 131 and 247.
282. *See* BATTESINI, *Direito e Economia, Novos Horizontes no Estudo da Responsabilidade Civil no Brasil*, 2011, São Paulo, at 251.

Chapter 2. Kinds of Damage

§1. INDIVIDUAL AND COLLECTIVE DAMAGE

199. Even though the Brazilian Civil Code of 2002 does not make any differentiation between individual and collective damages, these categories are present in the Brazilian system of torts, either by specific legislation or by doctrinal and jurisprudential construction. The Brazilian doctrine refers to individual harms as those that may affect people's physical, psychological, or moral integrity, or affect the property which comprises their patrimony. Collective harms, also denominated as trans-individual or supra-individual, are those that affect the property of a generic number of people that form a collective.[283]

200. A preoccupation with collective goods is one of the characteristics of the contemporary evolution of the Brazilian system of torts.[284] Law no. 4,717, of June 29, 1965, governs the popular class action, which legitimizes any citizen to ask for annulments or the declaration of nullities of acts harming the patrimony of the Union, the Federal District, the states or municipalities, as the respective members of the indirect administration specified in the legal text. Law no. 7,347, of July 24, 1985, governs civil class actions for environmental and consumer goods and values of an artistic nature, aesthetic, historical, tourist and landscape harms, attributing in its Article 5 legitimacy to the proposition of a legal suit to the Public Ministry, the Public Defender, the Union, the Federal District, the states, the municipalities, the autarchies, public firms, foundations, societies of mixed economy, and associations that fulfill the special requirements of a legal text. The objects of condemnation in civil class actions, according to Article 3 of the legal text, can consist in payment of damages, and obligations to do, or not to do, damages only being applicable when reparation *in natura* is not an option. The theme of collective moral harm has raised controversy on the jurisprudential plane. The First Group of the STJ has denied the application of collective moral harms based on the impossibility of determining the passive subject, the indivisibility of the offense, and therefore, the reparation.[285] On the other hand, the Second Group of the same court has admitted the concept of collective moral harm.[286]

§2. DIRECT AND INDIRECT

201. The Brazilian system of torts admits the reparation of harms caused directly to the victim, which are the immediate effect of the harmful fact, and the reparation of harms caused indirectly to the victim, which, not being immediately apparent,

---

283. *See* NORONHA, *Direito das Obrigações,* 2010, São Paulo, at 596.
284. *See* SCHREIBER, *Novos Paradigmas da Responsabilidade Civil,* 2009, São Paulo, at 84–85, and NADER, *Curso de Direito Civil, Responsabilidade Civil,* 2014, Rio de Janeiro, at 81–82.
285. *See* STJ, 1ª Turma, REsp 598.281/MG, Relator Ministro Luiz Fux, DJ. 01.06.2006, p. 147. Brasília.
286. *See* STJ, 2ª Turma, REsp 1.057.274/RS, Relatora Ministra Eliana Calmon, DJe. 26.02.2010. Brasília.

nonetheless have a connection to the harmful fact.[287] A special category of indirect harms are reflex or ricochet harms, in which the harmful fact, in addition to the direct victim, harms a third party who was also harmed by his/her connection to the victim of the harmful fact, such as a son who fails to receive sustenance by virtue of the death of his/her father in an accident. As happens with direct harms, indirect harms may be defined and certain or hypothetical or eventual.[288]

202. Under the influence of the civilian French doctrine, Brazilian jurisprudence has chosen the theory of loss of opportunity (*perte d'une chance*), a complex idea which, in a nutshell, allows the reparation of a harm caused by a harmful fact that suppresses the possibility of an event which may lead to a better future or avoid future loss to the victim. Loss of opportunity usually constitutes an indirect harm in which the author's liability depends on the configuration of the causation and the loss of a real opportunity and not a remote probability.[289] Loss of opportunity theory has been recognized by the STJ, being applied by the jurisprudence in situations such as loss of opportunity for adequate medical treatment caused by delay in the diagnosis of pathology,[290] and the loss of a chance to obtain a favorable legal decision, due to a deadline missed by an attorney.[291]

§3. Pecuniary and Non-pecuniary Losses

203. A distinction between material, also known as patrimonial or pecuniary, and moral harms, also known as extra-patrimonial or non-pecuniary, has as its starting point the concept of patrimony, understood as the bundle of goods of a person that are susceptible to economic evaluation in pecuniary terms. Therefore, in the doctrinal realm, it is understood that material harms are those that arise from the violation of interests connected to the patrimony of the victim, of specific economic interests, directly susceptible to pecuniary evaluation. On the other hand, moral harms are those that occur by the violation of the non-patrimonial interests of the victim, or that can be translated into a violation of interests not susceptible to pecuniary evaluation.[292]

204. The 2002 Brazilian Civil Code does not define material and moral harms, as it does not delimit the harms to be defended by the rule of law. Even so, the Brazilian system of torts reaches expressly applies to both modalities of harm, referring

---

287. *See* NORONHA, *Direito das Obrigações*, 2010, São Paulo, at 602–603.
288. *See* NADER, *Curso de Direito Civil, Responsabilidade Civil*, 2014, Rio de Janeiro, at 79–80.
289. *See* CAVALIERI FILHO, *Programa de Responsabilidade Civil*, 2012, São Paulo, at 77–81, and PEREIRA, *Responsabilidade Civil*, Rio de Janeiro, 2012, at 60–62.
290. *See* STJ, 3ª Turma, REsp 1.335.622/DF, Relator Ministro Ricardo Villas Bôas Cueva, DJe. 27.02.2013. Brasília.
291. *See* STJ, 4ª Turma, REsp 1.190.180/RS, Relator Ministro Luis Felipe Salomão, DJe. 22.11.2010. Brasília.
292. *See* NORONHA, *Direito das Obrigações*, 2010, São Paulo, at 590, and DINIZ, *Curso de Direito Civil Brasileiro, Responsabilidade Civil*, 2009, São Paulo, at 67–68 and 90–91.

in Article 5, V and X, and in the Article 114, VI, both from the Federal Constitution of 1988, and in Article 186 of the Civil Code of 2002, to moral harms as opposed to material harms.[293]

205. Material harms broadly encompass all the corporeal and non-corporeal things that comprise the patrimony of the victim, such as houses, vehicles, books, credit rights, etc. Moral harms, in their turn, are related to personality rights, such as good name, honor, liberty, physical integrity, image, intimacy and private life.[294] In practical terms, in the absence of objective criteria established in law, the relevant role in defining what is or is not moral harm is attributed to doctrine and jurisprudence.

206. In the doctrinal realm, the statement of Cavalieri Filho is paradigmatic[295] in the sense that the observation of "rules of good prudence, in the practical sense, of the just measure of things, of a complete weighing of the realities of life" is necessary for the characterization of moral harm. The author states his understanding that:

In this line of principle, only pain, harassment, and humiliation falling outside the norm, which interferes substantially with the psychological behavior of the individual, causing affliction, angst and disequilibrium to his well-being, can be considered a moral harm. Mere dislike, disturbances, upset, irritation or extreme sensibility are outside the scope of moral harm; aside from being part of our daily life's normality in work, traffic and between friends and even in a familiar environment, these situations are not sufficiently intense or lasting to affect the psychological equilibrium of the individual.

207. Jurisprudence identifies a wide spectrum of situations which characterize moral harm, referring to: the unauthorized use of photographic or cinematographic images;[296] injuries to physical integrity such as sight loss, amputation of members, an irreversible state of coma, aesthetic deformities, contamination by HIV in blood transfusions;[297] the occurrence of injuries to intimacy and private life by the press in order to obtain for legally protected information;[298] the incorrect inscription of

---

293. See FARIAS, BRAGA NETTO & ROSENVALD, *Novo Tratado de Responsabilidade Civil*, 2015, São Paulo, at 229, and NORONHA, *Direito das Obrigações*, 2010, São Paulo, at 590.
294. See NADER, *Curso de Direito Civil, Responsabilidade Civil*, 2014. Rio de Janeiro, at 84–87, and NORONHA, *Direito das Obrigações*, 2010, São Paulo, at 593.
295. See CAVALIERI FILHO, *Programa de Responsabilidade Civil*, 2012, São Paulo, at 86–87.
296. See STJ, 3ª Turma, REsp 1.323.586/PB, Relator Ministro Ricardo Villas Bôas Cueva, DJe. 11.03.2015; STJ, 2ª Turma, REsp 1.289.679/RS, Relatora Ministra Eliana Calmon, DJe. 18.09.2013. Brasilia.
297. See STJ, 2ª Turma, REsp 1.363.881/MG, Relator Ministro Herman Benjamin, DJe. 03.07.2014; STJ, 4ª Turma, REsp 1.248.206/SP, Relator Ministro Marco Buzzi, DJe. 20.08.2015; STJ, 3ª Turma, REsp 1.349.968/DF, Relator Ministro Marco Aurélio Bellizze, DJe. 14.04.2015; STJ, 4ª Turma, REsp 655.761/SP, Relator Ministro Marco Buzzi, DJe. 03.02.2015. Brasilia.
298. See STJ, 3ª Turma, REsp 1.380701/PA, Relator Ministro Marco Aurélio Bellizze, DJe. 14.05.2015. Brasilia.

legal or natural persons in a debtors' list;[299] the incorrect protest of a commercial title;[300] the publishing of libels by the press;[301] delays in the sending of university diploma;[302] lack of assistance to passenger in a flight delayed for more than four hours;[303] wrongful imprisonment arising from a legal mistake.[304] The STJ has supported the idea that damages for both material and moral harms are computable, even if they relate to the same fact.[305]

§4. PURE ECONOMIC LOSS

208. In the Brazilian legal system, pure economic loss is generally recoverable under the rules of contract law. Tort law does not generally allow compensation for pure economic loss. Pure economic interests are protected as such only by certain provisions, as is the case with Article 950 of the Brazilian Civil Code of 2002:

> if from the offense result defects by reason of which the injured person cannot exercise his job or profession, if his/her work capacity is diminished, the damage, in addition to the expenses of treatment and lost profits until the end of convalescence, will include a pension corresponding to the importance of the work for which he/her was disabled or suffered depreciation.

In environmental matters, with their basis in Article 14, paragraph 1, of Law no. 6,938/81, the reparation of pure economic losses caused to third parties is admitted, such as for example, with the payment of damages for restrictions on fishing activities through the emission of contaminants such as oil and mining effluents into rivers and seas.[306]

§5. ACTUAL AND FUTURE DAMAGE (LOST PROFITS)

209. Adopting as reference a particular temporal mark, such as the legal decision that determined the reparation, harms can be classified as present or current and future. If present harms have effectively occurred, these are verified at the time they are evaluated.[307] Briefly, the difference between current and future harms is present

---

299. *See* STJ, 4ª Turma, REsp 655.761/SP, Relator Ministro Marco Buzzi, DJe. 03.02.2015. Brasília.

300. *See* STJ, 3ª Turma, REsp 1.434.508/BA, Relator Ministro Sidnei Beneti, DJe. 04.06.2014. Brasília.

301. *See* STJ, 4ª Turma, REsp 1.365.284/SC, Luis Felipe Salomão, DJe. 21.10.2014. Brasília.

302. *See* STJ, 2ª Turma, REsp 1.524.143/PR, Relator Ministro Herman Benjamin, DJe. 30.06.2015. Brasília.

303. *See* STJ, 3ª Turma, REsp 1.280.372/SP, Relator Ministro Ricardo Villas Bôas Cueva, DJe. 10.10.2014. Brasília.

304. *See* STJ, 2ª Turma, REsp 1.385.946/MG, Relator Ministro Herman Benjamin, DJe. 15.04.2014. Brasilia.

305. *See* STJ, *súmula* nº 37. Brasilia.

306. *See* STJ, 2ª Seção, REsp 1.145.358/PR, Relator Ministro Ricardo Villas Bôas Cueva, DJe. 09.05.2012. Brasilia.

307. *See* FARIAS, BRAGA NETTO and ROSENVALD, *Novo Tratado de Responsabilidade Civil*, 2015, São Paulo, at 275, and NORONHA, *Direito das Obrigações*, São Paulo, 2010, at 603.

in the Brazilian system of torts. In terms of Article 402 of the Brazilian Civil Code, "pecuniary losses due to the creditor encompass, in addition to what he/she has effectively lost, the loss of reasonably anticipated profit." The effective losses of the victim, the diminution in patrimony caused by the harmful fact, constitute the emergent harms, for example, the material damage verified to a vehicle in a traffic accident. What the victim has ceased to profit from are the gains that, following the natural order of things, would probably have accrued to the patrimony of the victim if the harmful event had not occurred; this constitutes the ceasing of profits, for instance, the stopping of the earnings of a doctor, due to an accident that renders him or her incapable of exercising his/her profession for a determined period of time.[308]

§6. OTHER COSTS

210. In terms of the Brazilian Civil Procedure Code of 2015,[309] the costs of procedural expenses, such as the acts practiced in the proceeding and payment to experts (Article 82, §2, along with Article 84) fall to be paid by the defeated party, in addition to the payment of attorney fees to the winning party (Article 85). In a nutshell, attorney fees are given by the judge to a minimum of 10% and a maximum of 20% of the value of the judgment, of the economic profit or the current value of the cause (Article 85, §2). Differential treatment is assigned to the state observing a minimum of 1% and a maximum of 20% of the value of the conviction or economic advantage. In civil liability suits for illicit acts against persons, the fees will be applied to the sum of the due quotes added by twelve future quotes (Article 85, §9). In the case of reciprocal loss, the procedural expenses and attorney fees are proportionally distributed between the parties (Article 86).

§7. MITIGATION OF DAMAGES

211. The topic of mitigation of damages is not an object of legal prediction in the Brazilian legal system, even though, in some sense, mitigation of damages is considered an aspect of the injured party's contributory fault. In the terms of Article 945 of the Civil Code, "if the victim has concurred by fault with the harmful event, damages will be given according to the extent of his fault in the light of the agent's own fault."

---

308. *See* GONÇALVES, *Responsabilidade Civil*, 2006, São Paulo, at 652–653, and CAVALIERI FILHO, *Programa de Responsabilidade Civil*, 2012, São Paulo, at 74–75.
309. Law n. 13.105, of Mar. 16, 2015. Código de Processo Civil.

Chapter 3. Assessment and Compensation of Damages

§1. Objective Versus Subjective

212. Briefly, the assessment and compensation of damages is carried out by considering the value that the object would have for anybody. The value is determined by an objective method, usually by the market price. However, the specific value that the object has for the victim is considered by the Brazilian system of tort in specific situations, in the case of usurpation or divestment of property. According to the text of Article 952 of the Civil Code, "in order to restitute the equivalent, when the thing itself does not exist, its ordinary price and approximate value to the victim will be estimated, given that the latter does not exceed the former." Thus, the Brazilian legislator admits the subjective value to the victim in the case of usurpation or dispossession of property, but establishes an objective limitation, namely that the amount of compensation to be fixed for the emotional loss cannot be arbitrated as an amount higher than the market value of the thing in question.[310]

§2. Concrete Versus Abstract

213. Concerning assessment and compensation for harm in the Brazilian system of tort law, a distinction between concrete and abstract is usually not made. As a rule, the evaluation of and compensation for harms must be done in a concrete way. The term abstract is rarely used, but, could be suitable in cases of loss of opportunity and loss of profits, where the profits could have been expected with probability according to the particular circumstances or in the ordinary course of the events.

§3. Methods of Assessing Damages

214. In the Brazilian system of torts, the basic criterion or the value determination is given by the caput of Article 944 of the Civil Code, which is "the damages are given by the extent of the harm." This is, in essence, a positive statement of the *restitutio in integrum* principle, representing the ideal of seeking, as far as possible, the reinstatement of the victim to the situation prior to the harm suffered. The criterion of the extent of the harm is objective, and must guide the judicial actuation regarding the kind and portion to be paid by the debtor, in order to reestablish the equilibrium disturbed by the illegal misconduct.[311]

215. Regarding material damages, the difference theory is widely diffused, according to which the value due is given by the difference in the current value of the victim's patrimony and the value of the victim's patrimony if the harm had not

---

310. *See* GONÇALVES, *Responsabilidade Civil*, 2006, São Paulo, at 728–729, and NADER, *Curso de Direito Civil, Responsabilidade Civil*, 2014, Rio de Janeiro, at 221.
311. *See* GAMA, in: RODRIGUES JUNIOR, MAMEDE e ROCHA, *Responsabilidade Civil Contemporânea*, 2011, São Paulo, at 600–602.

occurred. The harm to the patrimonial value is given by the difference, considering the time of the harmful event and the time of the victim's compensation.[312] As a rule, the determination of the loss of patrimonial value is assessed by considering the market value of the goods.

216. As for moral harms, they follow the principle of compensatory satisfaction; the sum of pecuniary compensation to be due to the victim cannot assume the character of "price," but has a compensatory character for the suffering, physical or psychological pain, inflicted on the victim from the harm to his personality rights. Unlike the rules of material or patrimony harm, in which the market provides objective data for the determination of the damages, in the case of extra-patrimonial harms, the fixing of damages depends essentially on the equitable evaluation of the judiciary.[313] In the pecuniary quantification of compensation for moral harm, the judiciary has considered standards such as the economic standing of the author and the victim, the degree of fault of the author and the victim, the size of the harm, the circumstances of the event, the impact of the harm on the victim and the social repercussions of the event.[314] The setting of the value of the damages falls to the STJ,[315] which has acted as Libra in weighing the interests involved, valuing the balance of damages in a bundle of representative cases, such as the death of family members, incorrect inscription in debtors' lists, lies published in the press, illegal imprisonment, and unjustified flight cancelation.[316]

§4. EQUITABLE LIMITATION OF DAMAGES

217. The equitable limitation of damages in relation to the harm is admitted in the Brazilian system of torts, adopting as a basic criterion the degree of fault of the author and of the victim.[317] In addition to the basic rule of the symmetry between the damage and the harm predicted in the caput of Article 944, "the damage is given by the extent of the harm," the 2002 Brazilian Civil Code contains normative dispositions that expressly establish the reduction of the damages in proportion to the harm. Regarding the value of the damage reduction in relation to the harm, considering the degree of the author's and victim's fault, the sole paragraph of Article 944 of the Civil Code establishes that "if there is an excessive disproportion between

---

312. See NADER, *Curso de Direito Civil, Responsabilidade Civil*, 2014, Rio de Janeiro, at 84–85, and DINIZ, *Curso de Direito Civil Brasileiro, Responsabilidade Civil*, 2009, São Paulo, at 84–85 and 67–68.
313. See NADER, *Curso de Direito Civil, Responsabilidade Civil*, 2014, Rio de Janeiro, at 86–87, and NORONHA, *Direito das Obrigações*, São Paulo, 2010, at 593.
314. See STJ, 3ª Turma, AgRg no Ag 477.631/SP, Relator Ministro Carlos Alberto Menezes Direito, DJ. 31.03.2003, p. 224. Brasília.
315. See STJ, 4ª Turma, REsp 183.508/RJ, Relator Ministro Sálvio de Figueiredo Teixeira, DJ. 10.06.2002, p. 212, Brasília; STJ, 2ª Turma, REsp 487.749/RS, Relatora Ministra Eliana Calmon, DJ. 12.05.2003, p. 298. Brasília.
316. See RESEDÁ, *A Função Social do Dano Moral*, 2009, São José, at 214–219.
317. See BATTESINI, *Novos Horizontes no Estudo da Responsabilidade Civil no Brasil*, 2011, São Paulo, at 258–260, and TARTUCE, in: RODRIGUES JUNIOR, MAMEDE e ROCHA, *Responsabilidade Civil Contemporânea*, 2011, São Paulo, at 591–592.

the degree of fault degree and the harm, the judge can reduce the damages equitably." As for the reduction of the value of the damages in relation to the harm considering the concurrence of the degree of fault between the victim and the author, Article 945 of the Civil Code of 2002 establishes that "if the victim has concurred in the harmful event, his/her damages will be given taking into account the degree of fault accruing to the authors of the harm."

218. In reality, the notion of fault can be considered fundamental to the establishment of the imputation nexus, constituting the main principle that defines civil liability. More than that, the degree of fault of the author and the victim has an important role in the quantification of the value of damages. In this sense, while synthesizing the results of a comparative study developed by the European Centre of Tort Law and Insurance Law, *Unification of Tort Law: Fault*, Widmer[318] registers that the majority of legal systems do have some type of fault graduation, either "great negligence versus minimum negligence, passing through stages like 'medium' and 'simple' negligence to the lesser degree, the almost imperceptible fault (lighter fault)," highlighting that the degree of fault has a role in the "estimation of harms," without dispensing altogether with the "all or nothing principle followed by almost every system." In a certain sense, this road leads back to the traditional classification according to the degree of fault, originating from Roman law, and faults may be qualified as great, light and least. Where there is extreme negligence on the part of the agent this is considered as a great fault, in that he did not predict something predictable by the common man. It is considered a light fault where there was medium diligence, where the harm could have been avoided by an ordinary degree of attention. Finally, it is considered a slight fault when it occurs by lack of preventive conduct that transcends the medium standard, and the harm was caused by lack of an extraordinary degree of attention.[319]

219. Therefore, considering the Brazilian system of torts, the equitable reduction of damages in relation to the harm is admitted, in terms of the text of Article 944, when there is an excessive disproportion between the degree of fault of the agent and victim regarding the harm, or when a significant harm has been produced by conduct qualified as being a slight fault. Furthermore, an equitable reduction of damages regarding the harm is admitted, in terms of Article 945, when the victim has concurred in the harmful event, the idea being that the degree of the victim's fault is associated with its qualification as a slight, light or great fault, taking into consideration the author's own degree of fault.[320]

---

318. *See* WIDMER, *Unification of Tort Law: Fault*, 2005, The Hague, at 353.
319. *See* DINIZ, *Curso de Direito Civil Brasileiro, Responsabilidade Civil*, 2009, São Paulo, at 44, and CALIXTO, *A Culpa na Responsabilidade Civil, Estrutura e Função*, 2008, Rio de Janeiro, at 119.
320. *See* BATTESINI, *Novos Horizontes no Estudo da Responsabilidade Civil no Brasil*, 2011, São Paulo, at 263–264.

§5. METHODS OF PAYMENT

I. Lump Sum

220. The reparation of the harm can be specific, in species or *in natura*, forming the reinstatement of the situation prior to the harm, or it can be equivalent, through the delivery of pecuniary values to the victim. According to Article 947 of Brazilian Civil Code of 2002, the harm must usually be compensated in kind; however, "if the debtor cannot fulfill the debt in the adjusted species, it will be substituted by its value in current currency." In fact, the reparation by equivalency with the payment of a lump sum for all harms is the most common method of payment. In practical terms, in the course of the legal process the judge decides an amount in money, specifying an amount for the compensation of the harm, including emergent harm and profit loss, and moral harm.

II. Annuities

221. According to Article 950 of the Brazilian Civil Code of 2002, compensation through a monetary annuity is the regular remedy to be chosen if, as a consequence of injury to body or health, the earning capacity of the injured person is destroyed or impaired. In short, annuities are fixed in judgments, until the prospective time of retirement. In the terms of Article 950, sole paragraph, the victim may demand that the damages be paid in a lump sum. Another form of compensation is through monetary annuities, which is the payment of maintenance sums to the legal dependents of the victim who died in an accident, a possibility set out in Article 948, II, of the Civil Code. In both cases, the annuities can be reduced or increased according to the social and economic circumstances of the beneficiaries.

III. Others

222. The Brazilian system of torts allows, in specific situations, damages to be paid through the performance of specific acts intended for the mitigation of the consequences of the harm. This is the case of public disclosure in cases of injury, defamation or calumny (Article 953 of the Civil Code), which can be carried out by publishing a notice in the appropriate media.[321]

---

321. *See* FARIAS, BRAGA NETTO & ROSENVALD, *Novo Tratado de Responsabilidade Civil*, 2015, São Paulo, at 312–313.

Chapter 4. Personal Injury and Death

§1. PECUNIARY LOSSES

223. If a victim suffers an offense to health that results temporarily or permanently in a reduction in his/her work capacity, in the terms of Article 949 of the 2002s Brazilian Civil Code, the damages will consist in the payment of the treatment expenses (medical, chirurgical, residence, examinations, remedies, and other expenditure related to treatment of the harm), and of profit losses until the end of the treatment, apart from other harm that the victim may have suffered. If the offense results in a defect which means that the victim cannot carry on his/her job or work or reduces her/her work capacity, in the terms of Article 950, the damages will include the payment of a pension which will be fixed in value corresponding to the importance of the work for which the victim has been disabled or in the proportion to the reduction in his/her labor capacity.[322]

224. In the case of the victim's death, in the terms of Article 948, I and II, of the Civil Code, the damages will consist in the payment of treatment expenses, if the victim did not die immediately; expenses for the funeral and family mourning (mourning services, cremation, body preparation, etc.); as well as a pension to those for whose maintenance the victim was responsible, taking into account the probable life span of the victim. The pension will be fixed at two-thirds of the victims' earnings, given the assumption that one-third would be necessary for his/her living costs, if he/she was alive.[323] By jurisprudential construction, the pension is due to parents in the case of a deceased child[324] and is granted considering the victim's expected life span from the death date.[325] The math table of average life spans from the Brazilian population given by the Brazilian Institute of Geography and Statistics (Instituto Brasileiro de Geografia e Estatística) is used as a reference.[326] In addition, the pension due to children in case of their parents' decease ends at their 25th birthday, on the assumption that at this age they will have finished their academic studies (including university).[327]

---

322. *See* SENA, in: RODRIGUES JUNIOR, MAMEDE e ROCHA, *Responsabilidade Civil Contemporânea*, 2011, São Paulo, at 690–691, and CAVALIERI FILHO, *Programa de Responsabilidade Civil*, 2012, São Paulo, at 122–123.
323. *See* NANNI, in: Rodrigues JUNIOR, MAMEDE e ROCHA, *Responsabilidade Civil Contemporânea*, 2011, São Paulo, at 642–655, and CAVALIERI FILHO, *Programa de Responsabilidade Civil*, 2012, São Paulo, at 121–122.
324. *See* STJ, *súmula* nº 491. Brasília.
325. *See* STJ, 3ª Turma, AgRg no REsp 1.524.765/PE, Relator Ministro Paulo de Tarso Sanseverino, DJe. 07.10.2015. Brasília.
326. The expected life span for a newborn Brazil in 2014 was estimated to be 75 years and 2 months. *See Instituto Brasileiro de Geografia e Estatística – IBGE, Tábua Completa de Mortalidade*, Brasília, 2015. Available at pesquisa.in.gov.br.
327. *See* STJ, 3ª Turma, AgRg no REsp 1.529.730/RJ, Relator Ministro Ricardo Villa Bôas Cueva, DJe. 31.08.2015. Brasilia.

§2. NON-PECUNIARY LOSSES

225. In the case of body and health injury, according to Article 186 combined with Article 927 of the Brazilian Civil Code, in addition to pecuniary losses, the victim can demand monetary compensation for non-pecuniary losses or moral damages.[328] This is, in essence, compensation for suffering, physical or psychological pain inflicted on the victim, and is intended to ameliorate the consequences of the harmful event suffered by the victim.[329]

226. The understanding prevails in Brazilian doctrine and jurisprudence that moral damages fulfill a double function: from the victim's perspective, they act as compensation, providing satisfaction; and from the agent's perspective, they act as a punishment for the harm caused, the sanction function. As for the mixed character of the moral damages, the statement of Pereira is emblematic:

> in the reparation for moral harms is encompassed two reasons or two related causes: I) the punishment of the offender for the offense to a legal right of the victim, due its immateriality; II) to give to the offended a sum that is not a premium doloris, but a means to offer satisfaction of any nature, either intellectual or moral, or even material.[330]

The double function of moral damages is crystallized by the STJ, which attributes to the institute: a function to compensate the affected party for the harms suffered, aiming to minimize the victim's pain; and the pedagogic function, directed at the agent of the harmful act, to prevent similar events occurring in the future.[331]

227. In the scenario of the Brazilian torts system, the fixation of the amount of moral damages in cases of injury to body and health is a task delegated to the judiciary. As consolidated by the rationale of the STJ, moral damages are not the subject of tabulation:[332] they must be the object of the equitable appreciation of the judiciary. In the terms coined by Cavalieri Filho, "the principle of reasonable logic must be the compass of the judge. What is sensible, restrained and moderate is reasonable; a certain proportionality must be retained. Reasonableness is a criterion that allows the balancing of means and ends, causes and consequences, to reach a logical decision."[333] The STJ has admitted as a reasonable value in the case of

---

328. In the terms of the *Súmula* n° 37 of the Superior Court of Justice (*Superior Tribunal de Justiça*): "damages by material and moral harms originating from the same fact are commutable."
329. *See* ANDRADE, *Dano Moral e Indenização Punitiva: Os Punitive Damages na Experiência da Common Law e na Perspectiva do Direito Brasileiro*, 2009, Rio de Janeiro, at 149–150, and RESEDÁ, *A Função Social do Dano Moral*, 2009, São José, at 178–179.
330. *See* PEREIRA, *Responsabilidade Civil*, 2012, Rio de Janeiro, at 413.
331. *See* STJ, 1ª Turma, REsp 1.109.303/RS, Relator Ministro Luiz Fux, DJe. 05.08.2009. Brasília.
332. *See* STJ, *súmula* n° 281. Brasília.
333. *See* CAVALIERI FILHO, *Programa de Responsabilidade Civil*, 2012, São Paulo, at 98.

victim's death, the fixation of moral damages on a scale between 100 to 500 minimum wages, values between 22,000 to 110,000 American dollars or 19,800 to 98,900 euro,[334] according to the circumstances of the specific case.[335]

---

334. The minimum wage in Brazil in February 2016, was BRL 880 reais, equivalent to USD 220 American dollars or EUR 198 at the prevailing exchange rate.
335. *See* STJ, 1ª Turma, REsp 704.873/SP, Relatora Ministra Denise Arruda, DJ. 02.08.2007, p. 346 – damages of 100 minimum wages for her husband's murder in prison; STJ, 3ª Turma, REsp 329.979/MG, Relator Ministro Carlos Alberto Menezes Direito, DJ. 22.04.2002, p. 202 – indemnity of 200 minimum wages for his son's death in hospital; STJ, 1ª Turma, REsp 799.939/MG, Relator Ministro Luiz Fux, DJ. 30.08.2007 – compensation of 300 minimum wages for the death of a young person in a traffic accident with a school bus; STJ, 4ª Turma, REsp 1.279.173/SP, Relator Ministro Paulo de Tarso Sanseverino, DJe. 09.04.2013 – compensation of 400 minimum wages for the death of a young person falling from a train, and; STJ, 4ª Turma, REsp 223.545/SP, Relator Ministro Cesar Asfor Rocha, DJ. 26.06.2000, p. 179 – damages of 500 minimum wages for the death of a wife/mother in a traffic accident.

Chapter 5. Various Damages (Property)

228. In cases of property damage, the reparation must be specific, in species or *in natura*, being composed of the reinstatement of the factual prior situation regarding the harmful event, or of the delivery of equivalent pecuniary values to the victim. According to Article 947 of the Brazilian Civil Code of 2002, the harm must usually be compensated in kind; however, "if the debtor is not be able to fulfill the debt in the adjusted nature, it will be substituted by its value in current currency." In fact, equivalent compensation, with the payment given in money, is proper to originate a state of reality equivalent to that at the moment prior to the harm; this is the most common form of reparation for property harms.[336]

229. The calculation of patrimonial losses for the purposes of compensation is carried out considering the market values, of either the affected goods or the goods and services necessary to repair those harmed. If the object is lost or fully destroyed, the amount will be determined considering the current replacement value. For instance, in the case of motor vehicles, common use is made of a table by the Foundation Institute of Economics Researches (Fundação Instituto de Pesquisas Econômicas – FIPE), which gives the average prices of vehicles used on the national market, serving as a guide to valuation.[337] If the object is partially destroyed, the amount will be determined considering the costs of repair. Once more, considering the case of vehicles as a reference, the size of the amount necessary to repair the vehicle, generally, is calculated through the presentation of three quotations by trustworthy and capable firms, the lesser value being adopted.[338]

---

336. *See* NADER, *Curso de Direito Civil, Responsabilidade Civil*, 2014. Rio de Janeiro, at 84–85, and RIZZARDO, *Responsabilidade Civil*, 2007, Rio de Janeiro, at 53–56.
337. *See FUNDAÇÃO INSTITUTO DE PESQUISAS ECONÔMICAS, Tabela de Veículos Automotores.* Available at http://veiculos.fipe.org.br.
338. *See* NADER, *Curso de Direito Civil, Responsabilidade Civil*, 2014, Rio de Janeiro, at 217–218, and RIZZARDO, *Responsabilidade Civil*, 2007, Rio de Janeiro, at 59–62.

Chapter 6. Interference with Collateral Benefits

§1. INSURANCE

230. Private insurance is widespread in Brazil, either as first-party insurance or as third-party insurance, as voluntary insurance or as mandatory insurance. There are many modalities of insurance available in Brazil, particularly for patrimonial, personal, transportation and motor vehicle insurance.[339] A relatively new type of insurance, though already very popular, especially in the health care field, is civil liability insurance. With express legal establishment in Article 787 of 2002s Brazilian Civil Code, civil liability insurance is an institute by which the insured hires economic subrogation from the insurer for the obligations deriving from his/her liability for his/her actions during a determined activity.[340] Among the modalities of mandatory insurance, mandatory motor vehicle insurance, DPVAT, is highlighted. The vehicle's owner, when obtaining or renewing the vehicle's license, must take out the stipulated insurance in favor of third parties as potential accident victims.

231. In cases of civil liability, in brief, usually being demanded by the victim, the insured goes to the insurer, which will be obliged to pay damages to the victim up to the limits and on the conditions set out in the insurance contract. According to Article 781 of the Civil Code, the full price of the vehicle damaged can be paid by the insurance company, if it is equal to or less than the limits of the insured value, or the insurance company will offer partial damages for the vehicle, if the cover limit contracted is less than the verified harm. In the circumstance of partial cover, the insured will be responsible for the residual value due to the victim. In the event of the insolvency of the insurance company, the insured liability falls to the victim. By paying damages to the victim, the insurance company takes on itself the rights and actions that accrue to the insured against third parties, in the terms of Article 786 of the Civil Code.[341] Specifically, regarding mandatory insurance for motor vehicle owners, DPVAT, the victim is paid damages directly by the insurance company. If there is a legal dispute, as consolidated by the STJ, "the value of the mandatory insurance must be deducted from the legal damages fixed."[342]

§2. SOCIAL SECURITY AND MEDICARE

232. Brazil has a broad public system of social insurance, encompassing the health, social assistance, and providential care fields (Article 194 of the Federal

---

339. The regulation of the insurance markets, the open providence, capitalization and re-insurance in Brazil is made by the Private Insurances Superintendence (*Superintendência de Seguros Privados* – SUSEP). *See* www.susep.gov.br.
340. *See* SCHREIBER, *Novos Paradigmas da Responsabilidade Civil*, 2009, São Paulo, at 222–223.
341. *See* DINIZ, *Curso de Direito Civil. Responsabilidade Civil*, 2009, São Paulo, at 228–233.
342. *See Súmula* 246 do *Superior Tribunal de Justiça*. Brasília.

Constitution). In synthesis, the public health services (Article 196 of the Constitution) are universally accessible to the population, being financed by Brazilian society as a whole and headed jointly by the Union, states and municipalities, federated entities that comprise the sole health system (SUS) (Article 198 of the Federal Constitution). Public social assistance (Article 203 of the Constitution) is characterized by public financing and is headed jointly for the Union, states and municipalities for people who may need its services, including children, adolescents, the elderly and the disabled. To complete the public network, health and social assistance services are also offered by private entities. A wide spectrum of private health insurance is available.[343] As for public assistance, this includes the existence of a Special Social Assistance Regime for public servants (Article 40 of the Federal Constitution) and a General Social Assistance Regime for private workers (Article 201 of the Federal Constitution). Brazilian social assistance is characterized by its contributory character and mandatory affiliation, encompassing cover for events of sickness, disability, death, and old age. In addition to public assistance, private plans are also available.[344]

233. Social security has a significant impact on tort law, given that most victims of bodily injury are compensated for their own medical expenses, earning losses, and increased necessities by social security. As for the interface between civil liability and the public and private health systems, in a nutshell, the medical expenses of treating victims are paid by the public authorities and private entities, without damage payment by the harm's agent (negative externality), which is a common ground in traffic accidents, for instance. As for the interface between tort law and the public/private assistance system, of wide application is the "principle of accumulation of amounts" of a security nature with those of a compensatory nature.[345] The acknowledgment of Rizzardo's statement is mandatory for this topic: "The consolidation of the sum of pension, insurance and damage values in work accidents, with damages paid for different causes, is one of the most settled subjects in jurisprudence and doctrine; thus the nature of one does not confuse itself with the other."[346] On this particular subject, of labor accidents, the constitutional treatment of the Supreme Federal Court's (*Supremo Tribunal Federal*) is representative. According to Article 7, XXVIII, labor accident insurance, falling to the employer, does not exclude damages to which he/she is liable through intention or fault. In terms of Sumula 229 of the Supreme Federal Court, "accident damage payment does not exclude common rights, in the case of intention or severe fault by the employer."[347]

---

343. The regulation of complementary health plans is carried out by the National Health Agency (*Agência Nacional de Saúde Suplementar* – ANS). *See* www.ans.gov.br.
344. Insurance market regulation, open providence, capitalization and re-insurance in Brazil is carried out by the Private Insurance Superintendence (*Superintendência de Seguros Privados* – SUSEP). *See* www.susep.gov.br.
345. *See* GONÇALVES, *Responsabilidade Civil*, 2006, São Paulo, at 812–813.
346. *See* RIZZARDO, *Responsabilidade Civil*, 2007, Rio de Janeiro, at 908.
347. *See Súmula* 229 do *Supremo Tribunal Federal*. Brasília.

§3. OTHERS

234. As well as insurance and social security benefits, the victim may receive monetary benefits derived from other sources. In this case, such benefits may result in a reduction of the victim's claim in order to take account of the benefits received from those sources, depending on the court's rationale and the specific law applicable to such cases.

Chapter 7. Other Remedies

§1. Restitution (For Unjust Enrichment)

235. Unjust enrichment is the object of regulation in Chapter 4, Title VII – Unilateral Acts, of the Obligations Book of the 2002 Brazilian Civil Code. In terms of Article 884, "a person who, without just cause, enriches him/herself at the cost of other, will be obliged to restitute the undue amount acquired." In essence, unjust enrichment is a patrimonial advantage acquired by a subject of rights without a legal basis, implying for the subject who obtains the patrimonial advantage the need to compensate the subject harmed. In contraposition to civil liability, which has as its main end to restore the patrimonial reduction of a creditor, by the reparation of harms, action against unjust enrichment has as its goal to remove from the third party's patrimony the undue credits, restoring them to the creditor.[348] In brief, considering the idea of damage evaluation, there is a fine line between patrimonial compensation and the unjust enrichment of the victim. This situation has relevance in moral damages; thus doctrine and jurisprudence in Brazil admits that, in addition to the compensatory function, the quantification of damages should take into account the punitive and pedagogic functions.[349]

§2. Injunctive Relief

236. Injunctive relief is the object of Title II, Book V – Provisory Remedy, from the Brazilian Procedure Civil Code of 2015, and it can be allowed by the judiciary, in the terms of Article 300 of the Procedure Code, "when there are elements that point to the probability of a right and danger of harm or risk to the useful result of the process." Even though the 2002 Brazilian Civil Code does not contemplate specific situations of civil liability that may justify the urgent remedy, it can be used by victims of illicit acts in situations in which is necessary for the judiciary to order a person to do something or to stop doing something connected with a harmful situation.

§3. Punitive Damages

237. In synthesis, under the rules of Brazilian tort law, damages have a compensatory nature. The objective of the tort law system is to put the victim in the same position that he would be in if the illicit act had not taken place. Therefore, as occurs

---

348. *See* NORONHA, *Direito das Obrigações*, 2010, São Paulo, at 443–444, and COELHO, *Curso de Direito Civil, Responsabilidade Civil*, 2005, São Paulo, at 243–244.
349. *See* §2. Non-pecuniary losses, Chapter 4. Personal Injury and Death, Part VI. Remedies.

in the great majority of civil law tradition countries, by the lack of specific prediction, punitive damages are not admitted in Brazilian tort law.[350] In this sense, as Calixto has it:[351]

> the base-norm of the idea of reparation for harm still lies in Article 944, of the Civil Code's caput, according to which "the damages are determined by the extent of the harm". Reduction of the damages value can be admitted, though … on the other hand, it an increase in compensation values can be admitted as a deterrent to the offender's behavior in the case of specific legislation – which is not present in the current Civil Code.

238. Gradually, though, under influence of the common law, the punitive damages theme has been debated in the field of Brazilian tort law. There is a consistent national doctrine that defends the application of punitive damages through moral damages, taking its basis from constitutional principles, a comprehension that has been implicitly accepted by jurisprudence.[352] In this sense, as Andrade states:[353]

> the Brazilian Civil Code does not contemplate expressly the application of damages in their punitive nature. On the contrary, the general rule is given by the Article 944 that established that the extent of the harm provides limits to damages … Independent of any legal prediction, punitive damages in moral damages are applicable in our legal ordainment, which bases them on constitutional principles.

---

350. *See* BATTESINI, Negligence, Hand Formula and Compensation, 2013. New York, SSRN, at 14–15, http://ssrn.com/abstract=1988935.
351. *See* CALIXTO, *A Culpa na Responsabilidade Civil, Estrutura e Função*, 2008, Rio de Janeiro, at 309–310.
352. *See* §2. Non-pecuniary losses, Ch. 4. Personal Injury and Death, Part VI. Remedies.
353. *See* ANDRADE, *Dano Moral e Indenização Punitiva: Os Punitive Damages na Experiência da Common Law e na Perspectiva do Direito Brasileiro*, 2009, Rio de Janeiro, at 236–237.

Selected Bibliography

General Bibliography

AGGIO, Alberto. Política e sociedade no Brasil, 1930–1964. São Paulo: Annablume, 2002.

BARBOSA, Rui. A raiz das coisas: o Brasil no mundo. São Paulo: Civilização Brasileira, 2008.

BARCELLOS, Marta & AZEVEDO, Simone. Histórias do Mercado de Capitais no Brasil. São Paulo: Campus Elsevier, 2011.

BOXER, Charles R. IMPÉRIO MARÍTIMO PORTUGUÊS – 1415–1825. São Paulo: Companhia das Letras, 2011.

BRAD SHAW FOUNDATION. "Journey of mankind." Retrieved November 17, 2009. Available at http://www.bradshawfoundation.com/stephenoppenheimer/index.php.

BUENO, Eduardo. Brasil uma História. São Paulo: Editora Ática, 2004.

CUNHA, Manuela Carneiro. História dos Índios no Brasil. São Paulo: Companhia das Letras, 1992.

ESTADO DE SÃO PAULO, "A vitória de Dilma." Available at http://www.estadao.com.br/estadaodehoje/20101102/not_imp633577,0.php.

ETHNOLOGUE. Languages of the World. Available at http://www.ethnologue.com/country/br and CENSUS, IBGE. Available at http://censo2010.ibge.gov.br/apps/atlas.

FAUSTO, Boris e DEVOTO Fernando J. Devoto. História do Brasil. São Paulo: Sebo Avalovara, 2004.

FILIPPI, Eduardo Ernesto. Evolução econômica e institucional do setor primário no Brasil: em direção ao desenvolvimento rural? Maputo, 2006.

G1. "Manifestações contra o Governo Dilma ocorrem pelo País." Available at http://g1.globo.com/politica/noticia/2016/03/manifestacoes-contra-governo-dilma-ocorrem-pelopais.html.

GASPARI, Elio. A ditadura escancarada. São Paulo: Companhia das Letras, 2002.

GOMES, Marco Antônio Ferreira, FRIZOLA, Heloisa Ferreira and SPADOTTO, Cláudio. Revista Do Departamento De Geografia, 18 (2006) 67–74. "CLASSIFICAÇÃO DAS ÁREAS DE RECARGA DO SISTEMA AQÜÍFERO GUARANI NO BRASIL EM DOMÍNIOS PEDOMORFOAGROCLIMÁTICOS – SUBSÍDIO AOS ESTUDOS DE AVALIAÇÃO DE RISCO DE CONTAMINAÇÃO DAS ÁGUAS SUBTERRÂNEAS." CLASSIFICAÇÃO DAS ÁREAS DE RECARGA DO SISTEMA AQÜÍFERO GUARANI NO BRASIL EM

Selected Bibliography

DOMÍNIOS PEDOMORFOAGROCLIMÁTICOS – SUBSÍDIO AOS ESTU-
DOS DE AVALIAÇÃO DE RISCO DE CONTAMINAŞÃO DAS ÁGUAS (n.d.):
n. pag. October 2005. Web. Available at https://www.embrapa.br/busca-de-
publicacoes/-/publicacao/15909/classificacao-das-areas-de-recarga-do-sistema-
aquifero-guarani-no-brasil-em-dominios-pedomorfoagroclimaticos---subsidios-
aos-estudos-de-avaliacao-do-risco-de-contaminacao-das-aguas-subterraneas.

GUTTENBERG, Pacheco Lopes Junior. "The Sino-Brazilian Principles in a Latin
American and BRICS Context: The Case for Comparative Public Budgeting
Legal Research." Wisconsin International Law Journal. May 13, 2015. Retrieved
6 June, Madison, 2015.

HERNANI, Donato. Dicionário das Batalhas Brasileiras. São Paulo: Ibrasa, 1996.

HOLANDA, Sérgio Buarque, CAMPOS, Pedro Moacyr and FAUSTO, Boris.
História geral da civilização brasileira. São Paulo: Difusão Européia.

IBGE, *Instituto Brasileiro de Geografia e Economia* (Brazilian Institute for
Geografic and Economic Data). 2010 IBGE's Census. Available at www.ibge-
.gov.br.

LEAL, Victor Nunes. Coronelismo, Enxada e Voto: o município e o sistema representativo no Brasil. São Paulo: Companhia das Letras, 1949.

LYRA, Heitor. História de Dom Pedro II (1825–1891): Ascenção (1825–1870) 1.
História de Dom Pedro II (1825–1891): Fastígio (1870–1880) 2. História de Dom
Pedro II (1825–1891): Declínio (1880–1891) 3 (in Portuguese). Belo Horizonte:
Itatiaia, 1977.

LUSTOSA, Isabel. D. Pedro I – um herói sem nenhum caráter. São Paulo: Cia. das
Letras, 2006.

MELLO, Christiane Figueiredo Pagano. "Forças Militares no Brasil Colonial."
E-papers 2009 ISBN 9788576502050. Rio de Janeiro. Available at http://www.e
-papers.com.br/produtos.asp?codigo_produto=1667.

MENDONÇA, Daniel. Tancredo Neves – Da Distensão à Nova República. Santa
Cruz do Sul: Edunisc, 2004.

MERCOSUR. Acerca del MERCOSUR. Available at www.mercosur.int.

MOSHER, Jeffrey C. Political Struggle, Ideology, and State Building: Pernambuco
and the Construction of Brazil, 1817–1850. 2008 [S.l.]: University of Nebraska
Press. Lincoln.

MSN. ENCARTA. "Plant and Animal Life." MSN. Archived from the original on
October 31, 2009. Retrieved 12 June, 2008.

MSN. ENCARTA,/. "Environmental Issues." MSN. Archived from the original on
October 31, 2009. Retrieved 12 June, 2008.

Observatório Nacional de Segurança Viária – ONSV, Retrato da Segurança Viária
no Brasil, Brasília, 2014. Available at http://onsv.org.br.

PAIVA, Denise. Era outra história: política social do governo Itamar Franco
1992–1994. Juiz de Fora, Editora UFJF, 2009.

PENNA, Lincoln de Abreu. O progresso da ordem: O florianismo e a construção da
República. Rio de Janeiro, 2008.

PORTAL TERRA. Governo brasileiro é pressionado por históricos protestos (June
21, 2013). Available at http://noticias.terra.com.br/brasil/governo-brasileiro-e-
pressionado-por-historicos.protestos,f614e49fccf5f310VgnCLD2000000ec6eb0
aRCRD.html.

PRADO, Maria Ligia. A Formação das Nações Latino-Americanas. Campinas, 1986.
RODRIGUEZ, José Honório & Ricardo A.S. Seitenfus. Leda Boechat Rodrigues. História Diplomática do Brasil, 1995. São Paulo.
SEITENFUS, Ricardo AS. "2.2," A entrada do Brasil na Segunda Guerra Mundial. Porto Alegre: EdiPUCRS, 2000.
SKIDMORE, Thomas. História Geral. Recife: Livraria Progresso Sebo 2003.
THE ECONOMIST (2012). Democracy Index Economist Intelligence Unit. Visited on June 21, 2013.
THE ECONOMIST (2010). Democracy Index Economist Intelligence Unit. Visited on June 21, 2013.
VIANNA, Hélio. "História do Brasil: período colonial, monarquia e república." 15. ed. São Paulo: Melhoramentos, 1994.

Legal Bibliography

ACCIARRI, Hugo. La Relación de Causalidad y las Funciones del Derecho de Daños. Buenos Aires: Abeledo Perrot, 2009.
ANDRADE, André Gustavo Corrêa de. Dano moral e indenização punitiva: os punitive damages na experiência do common law e na perspectiva do direito brasileiro. 2ª ed. Rio de Janeiro: Lumen Juris, 2009.
BATTESINI, Eugênio. Direito e Economia, Novos Horizontes no Estudo da Responsabilidade Civil no Brasil. São Paulo: LTr, 2011.
BATTESINI, Eugênio. Negligence, Hand Formula, and Compensation (January 20, 2012). Available at SSRN: http://ssrn.com/abstract=1988935 or http://dx.doi.org /10.2139/ssrn.1988935.
BATTESINI, Eugênio. Comparison of Tort Law Systems from the Perspective of Economic Efficiency: Brazilian Civil Code, Principles of European Law and Restatements of the Law (April 17, 2015). Available at SSRN: http://ssrn.com/ abstract=2595790 or http://dx.doi.org/10.2139/ssrn.2595790.
BATTESINI, Eugênio. Tort Law and Economic Development: Strict Liability in Legal Practice, ALACDE, 2015. Available at ALACDE: http://laijle.alacde.org/ journal/vol1/iss1/2.
BENJAMIN, Antônio Hermann. O Código de Defesa do Consumidor. 10 ª ed. Rio de Janeiro: Forense Universitária, 2011.
BITTAR, Carlos Alberto. Responsabilidade civil: teoria e prática. 2. ed. Rio de Janeiro: Forense Universitária, 1990.
BORGES, Gustavo. Erro Médico nas Cirurgias Plásticas. São Paulo: Atlas, 2014.
BOUKAERT, Boudewijn and DE GEEST, Gerrit (org.). Encyclopedia of Law and Economics. Cheltenham: Edward Elgar, 2009.
CALIXTO, Marcelo Junqueira. A Culpa na Responsabilidade Civil, Estrutura e Função. Rio de Janeiro: Renovar, 2008.
CAMPINHO, Sérgio. O Direito da Empresa à luz no Novo Código Civil. 11ª ed. Rio de Janeiro: Renovar, 2010.
CANOTILHO, J.J. Gomes; MENDES, Gilmar Ferreira; SARLET, Ingo Wolfgang; STRECK, Lenio (Coord.). Comentários à Constituição do Brasil. São Paulo: Saraiva/Almedina, 2013.

Selected Bibliography

CAVALIERI FILHO, Sérgio. Programa de Responsabilidade Civil. 9ª ed. São Paulo: Atlas, 2010.

COELHO, Fábio Ulhoa. Curso de Direito Civil – Responsabilidade Civil. 2ª ed. São Paulo: Saraiva, 2005.

COELHO, Inocêncio Martires, in CANOTILHO, J. J. Gomes; MENDES, Gilmar Ferreira; SARLET, Ingo Wolfgang; STRECK, Lenio (Coord.). Comentários à Constituição do Brasil. São Paulo: Saraiva/Almedina, 2013.

COOTER, Robert and ULEN, Thomas. Law and Economics. 5ª ed. Pearson Education, 2008. Boston.

CRUZ, Gisela Sampaio da. O Problema do Nexo Causal na Responsabilidade Civil. Rio de Janeiro: Renovar, 2005.

DAM, Cees Van. European Tort Law. Oxford: Oxford University Press, 2006.

DIAS, José de Aguiar. Cláusula de não-indenizar. 4ª ed. Rio de Janeiro: Forense, 1980.

DIAS, José de Aguiar. Da Responsabilidade Civil. 11ª ed. Renovar, 2006. Rio de Janeiro.

DINIZ, Maria Helena. Curso de direito civil brasileiro. V. 7. Responsabilidade Civil. 19. ed. São Paulo: Saraiva, 2009.

DIREITO, Carlos Alberto Menezes and CAVALIERI FILHO, Sérgio. Comentários ao Novo Código Civil, V. XIII, Da Responsabilidade Civil, Das Preferências e Privilégios Creditórios. 2ª ed. Rio de Janeiro: Forense, 2007.

FACHINI NETO, Eugênio. Da Responsabilidade Civil no Novo Código. In. SARLET, Ingo W. (org.). O Novo Código Civil e a Constituição. 2ª ed. Porto Alegre: Livraria do Advogado, 2006.

FARIAS, Cristiano Chaves; BRAGA NETTO, Felipe Peixoto; and ROSENVALD, Nelson. Novo Tratado de Responsabilidade Civil. São Paulo: Atlas, 2015.

FIÚZA, César Augusto de Castro. Direito civil. Curso completo. 14. ed. Belo Horizonte: Del Rey, 2010.

GAMA, Guilherme Calmon Nogueira. Critérios de Valoração da Indenização, Obrigação Indeterminada e Substituição do Valor da Indenização. In: RODRIGUES JUNIOR, Otávio Luiz, MAMEDE, Gladston, and ROCHA, Maria Vital. Responsabilidade Civil Contemporânea. São Paulo: Atlas, 2011.

GONÇALVES, Carlos Roberto. Responsabilidade Civil. 9ª ed. São Paulo: Saraiva, 2006.

GONÇALVES, Carlos Roberto. Direito Civil Brasileiro, vol. 4. São Paulo: Saraiva, 2007.

HART, H.L.A. & HONORÉ, Tony. Causation in the Law. Oxford: Oxford University Press, 1959.

KOCH, Bernhard A. and KOZIOL, Helmut. Comparative Conclusions. In KOCH, Bernhard A. and KOZIOL, Unification of Tort Law: Strict Liability. The Hague: Kluwer Law International, 2002. Principles of European Tort Law, vol. 6, European Centre of Tort Law and Insurance Law.

LIMA, Alvino. A responsabilidade civil pelo fato de outrem. Rio de Janeiro: Ed. Borsoi, 1972.

LISBOA, Roberto Senise. Manual de Direito Civil, vol. 2 – Obrigações e Responsabilidade Civil. 3ª ed. São Paulo: Revista dos Tribunais, 2004.

LÔBO, Paulo. Direito Civil – Contratos. São Paulo: Saraiva, 2011.

Selected Bibliography

MELLO, Marcos Bernardes. Teoria do Fato Jurídico – Plano da Existência. 12ª ed. São Paulo: Saraiva, 2003.

MIRAGEM, Bruno. Abuso do Direito = Proteção da Confiança e Limite ao Exercício das Prerrogativas Jurídicas no Direito Privado. Rio de Janeiro: Forense, 2009.

MIRANDA, Francisco C. Pontes de. Atualização: Vilson Rodrigues Alves. Tratado de direito privado. Campinas: Bookseller Editora, 2003.

MORAES, Maria Celina Bodin de. Danos à pessoa humana: uma leitura civil- constitucional dos danos extrapatrimoniais. São Paulo: Renovar, 2003.

NADER, Paulo. Curso de Direito Civil, vol. 7 – Responsabilidade Civil. 5ª ed. Rio de Janeiro: Forense, 2014.

NANNI, Giovanni Ettore. Indenização e Homicídio. In RODRIGUES JUNIOR, Otávio Luiz, MAMEDE, Gladston, and ROCHA, Maria Vital. Responsabilidade Civil Contemporânea. São Paulo: Atlas, 2011.

NORONHA, Fernando. Direito das Obrigações. 3ª ed. São Paulo: Saraiva, 2010.

NOVO CÓDIGO CIVIL BRASILEIRO, Lei nº 10.406, de 10 de janeiro de 2002: Estudo Comparativo com o Código de 1916, Constituição Federal, Legislação Codificada e Extravagante. 4ª ed. São Paulo: Revista dos Tribunais, 2004.

PAULA, Carolina Bellini Arantes. As excludentes de Responsabilidade Civil Objetiva. São Paulo: Atlas, 2007.

PASTOR, Santos. Derecho de Daños. In. SPECTOR, Horacio (org.). Elementos de Análisis Económico del Derecho. Buenos Aires: Rubinzal-Culzoni Editores, 2004.

PEREIRA, Caio Mário da Silva. Responsabilidade Civil. 10ª ed. Rio de Janeiro: GZ Editora, 2012.

PINTO, Paulo Mota. Sobre Condição e Causa na Responsabilidade Civil. "Estudos em Homenagem ao Professor Doutor António Castanheira Neves," v. III: Direito Público, Direito Penal e História do Direito. Coimbra: Ed. Coimbra, 2008.

RAZ, Joseph. Practical Reasons and Norms. Oxford: Oxford University Press, 1999.

REALE, Miguel. Diretrizes Gerais sobre o Projeto de Código Civil. In REALE, Estudos de Filosofia e Ciência do Direito. São Paulo: Saraiva, 1978.

REALE, Miguel. Visão Geral do Novo Código Civil. In NOVO CÓDIGO CIVIL BRASILEIRO, Lei nº 10.406, de 10 de janeiro de 2002: Estudo Comparativo com o Código de 1916, Constituição Federal, Legislação Codificada e Extravagante. 4ª ed. São Paulo: Revista dos Tribunais, 2004.

RESEDA, Salomão. A Função Social do Dano Moral. Florianópolis: Conceito Editorial, 2009.

RIZZARDO, Arnaldo. Responsabilidade Civil. 3ª ed. Rio de Janeiro: Forense, 2007.

RODRIGUES, Sílvio. Direito Civil, vol. 4 – Responsabilidade Civil. 19ª ed. São Paulo: Saraiva, 2002.

RODRIGUES JUNIOR, Otávio Luiz, MAMEDE, Gladston, and ROCHA, Maria Vital. Responsabilidade Civil Contemporânea. São Paulo: Atlas, 2011.

SANSEVERINO, Paulo de Tarso Vieira. Princípio da Reparação Integral. São Paulo: Saraiva, 2013.

SANTOLIM, Cesar. Nexo de Causalidade e Prevenção na Responsabilidade Civil, Revista da AJURIS – v. 41 – n. 136 – December 2014. Porto Alegre.

Selected Bibliography

SARLET, Ingo W. (org.). O Novo Código Civil e a Constituição. 2ª ed. Porto Alegre: Livraria do Advogado, 2006.

SENA, Adriana Goulart. Indenização e Perda da Capacidade Laborativa. In RODRIGUES JUNIOR, Otávio Luiz, MAMEDE, Gladston, and ROCHA, Maria Vital. Responsabilidade Civil Contemporânea. São Paulo: Atlas, 2011.

SCHÄFER, Hand-Bernd and OTT, Claus. The Economic Analysis of Civil Law. Cheltenham: Edward Elgar, 2004.

SCHÄFER, Hans-Bernd and Müller-Langer, Strict Liability versus Negligence, in: BOUKAERT, Boudewijn and DE GEEST, Gerrit (org.). Encyclopedia of Law and Economics. Cheltenham: Edward Elgar, 2009.

SCHREIBER, Anderson. Novos Paradigmas da Responsabilidade Civil, da Erosão dos Filtros da Reparação à Diluição dos Danos. 2ª ed. São Paulo: Atlas, 2009.

SEVERO, Sérgio. Tratado da Responsabilidade Pública. São Paulo: Saraiva, 2009.

SHAVELL, Steven. Foundations of Economic Analysis of Law. Cambridge: Harvard University Press, 2004.

SILVA, De Plácido. Vocabulário Jurídico. Rio de Janeiro: Forense, 2008.

SILVA, Wilson Melo da. O dano moral e sua reparação. Rio de Janeiro: Forense, 1969.

SPECTOR, Horácio (org.). Elementos de Análisis Económico del Derecho. Buenos Aires: Rubinzal-Culzoni Editores, 2004.

STOCO, Rui. Tratado de Responsabilidade Civil. 10 ª ed. São Paulo: Revista dos Tribunais, 2014.

TARTUCE, Flávio. Redução Equitativa da Indenização. In RODRIGUES JUNIOR, Otávio Luiz, MAMEDE, Gladston, and ROCHA, Maria Vital. Responsabilidade Civil Contemporânea. São Paulo: Atlas, 2011.

TESTA, Matias Yrigoñen, Daños Punitivos, Análisis Económico del Derecho y Teoría de Juegos. Buenos Aires, 2006.

THEODORO JUNIOR, Humberto. Comentários ao Novo Código Civil. 2ª ed. Rio de Janeiro: Forense, 2003.

VENTURI, Thaís Goveia Pascoaloto. Responsabilidade Civil Preventiva. São Paulo: Malheiros, 2014.

WALD, Arnold. Direito Civil. V. 7. Obrigações e Contratos. São Paulo: Saraiva, 2009.

WERRO, Franz, PALMER, Vernon V. Strict Liability in European Tort Law: An Introduction. In WERRO, Franz, PALMER, Vernon V. (ed.). The Boundaries of Strict Liability in European Tort Law. Durham: Carolina Academic Press, 2004.

WIDMER, Pierre. Comparative Report on Fault as a Basis of Liability and Criterion of Imputation (Attribution). In WIDMER, Pierre (ed.) Unification of Tort Law: Fault. The Hague: Kluwer Law International, 2005. Principles of European Tort Law, vol. 10. European Centre of Tort Law and Insurance Law.

ZWEIGERT, Konrad and KÖTZ, Hein. Introducción al Derecho Comparado. Mexico: Oxford University Press, 2002.

Index

The numbers here refer to paragraph numbers.

Index